CHICAGO

31

UNSUNG HEROES
OF
PRO BASKETBALL

Exciting profiles of nine "Cinderella" cagers whose unique contributions to their teams often went unnoticed. Included are these ABA and NBA stars: Mel Daniels, Bob Love, Dan Issel, Hal Greer, Dave DeBusschere, Roger Brown, Lenny Wilkens, Charlie Scott and Gus Johnson.

UNSUNG HEROES
OF
PRO BASKETBALL

by Ray Hill

illustrated with photographs

Random House

PRO
BASKETBALL
LIBRARY

New York

To Lou Sabin, who pointed me toward the hoop

Copyright © 1973 by Random House, Inc.
All rights reserved under International and Pan-American Copyright Conventions. Published in the United States by Random House, Inc., New York, and simultaneously in Canada by Random House of Canada Limited, Toronto.
Manufactured in the United States of America

Library of Congress Cataloging in Publication Data
Hill, Ray.
Unsung heroes of pro basketball.
(Pro basketball library)
    SUMMARY: Brief biographies of nine basketball players including Mel Daniels, Bob Love, Dan Issel, Hal Greer, Dave DeBusschere, Roger Brown, Lenny Wilkens, Charlie Scott, and Gus Johnson.
    1. Basketball—Biography—Juvenile literature.
[1. Basketball—Biography]   I. Title.
GV884.A1H5   796.32'3'0922 [920]   73-4233
ISBN 0-394-82415-6   ISBN 0-394-92415-0 (lib. bdg.)

CONTENTS

INTRODUCTION

Not every pro basketball star gets the credit he deserves. And that's what this book is all about: nine outstanding players who have suffered from a lack of recognition.

The men represented here play in both the American and National Basketball Leagues. Some are just reaching their playing primes, while others are near the end of great careers. But for one reason or another, their contributions have been underrated.

Dave DeBusschere and Hal Greer both played with NBA champions, but often they were overshadowed by the flashy superstars on their teams.

Lenny Wilkens was always a quiet leader, never one to grab the spotlight.

Bob Love sat on the benches of three NBA clubs before anyone gave him a chance. It wasn't until the 1972–73 season that he began to get his fair share of publicity.

Charlie Scott's outspoken personality was most often the subject of the stories written about him. His fine on-the-court achievements were usually pushed into the background.

Mel Daniels, Dan Issel and Roger Brown, a trio of ABA super-players, were virtually unknown to many fans because their league never got the kind of coverage that was given to the more established NBA.

Gus Johnson, who spent his most productive years in the NBA, got off to a dazzling start as a pro but was plagued by injuries at the peak of his notable career.

No, these weren't pro basketball's only unsung heroes. There were many others like them. Perhaps in some future book they, too, will be recognized.

I wish to thank Nick Curran, NBA public relations head, and *Sport* Magazine for the unlimited use of their files.

1.

Mel Daniels

It was the sixth game of the 1972 championship ABA playoffs: Indiana vs. New York at the Nets' Nassau Coliseum. The Pacers were ahead three games to two in the best-of-seven series. But all was not well. Indiana's super-center, Mel Daniels, was not having a good series. In the first four matches he had been outplayed by Bill Paultz, New York's young 6-foot-11 pivotman. To make matters worse, Daniels had sprained his ankle in the fourth game.

By game six the ankle was swollen to twice its normal size, and it looked as if Mel might have to sit that one out. But he played. He played 31 of the longest, most painful minutes in his life.

Mel Daniels and Billy Paultz (#5) are the two big men as the Pacers meet the New York Nets in the 1972 ABA playoffs.

The pain increased with every step Mel took. When he pivoted on the ankle or came down hard with a rebound, it was so bad it almost brought tears to his eyes. Yet the Indiana center kept himself right in the middle of the action—setting picks, grabbing rebounds, harrassing Paultz on defense.

By the fourth quarter Mel was hobbling up and down the court, desperately trying to stay in the flow of play. The hometown crowd shouted to Paultz: "Work on him! The guy can't walk!"

True, he couldn't walk too well—but Daniels could still shoot. He scored nine points in the period (including two foul-line jump shots) to give Indiana an eleven-point lead. To top it off, he crushed a late New York rally by snagging a rebound and freezing the ball until the buzzer. When the game ended Mel had 18 points and 12 rebounds, and the Pacers had their second ABA title.

"The adrenalin was really flowing," he said after the game. "You can't bother with pain at a time like that. This is a championship, and there's nothing like a championship. Nothing."

And there was no one like Mel Daniels. Although many NBA fans had never even heard of Daniels, for years he was the most honored player in the ABA. In his first five years in the league he was Rookie of the Year and twice Most Valuable Player, and he held the career record for rebounds. He played in every All-Star game and received

MVP honors there. In addition, he was named to the All-ABA first team three times.

If Daniels never got as much publicity as many NBA stars, it was only because the ABA had gotten far less attention from sportswriters and television than the older NBA. "It's really disheartening," he said, "to look at the literature and see us pushed back to the end of the magazines, while up front you see all about 'the great NBA players.'"

Daniels recalled the night the New York Knicks won the 1969–70 NBA title. The game was carried on national television, and Daniels didn't like what he saw. "That Howard Cosell has got to go!" Mel complained. "When he announced after the Knicks had beaten the Lakers, 'You are truly the world champions of professional basketball,' I had to turn off the TV. He had his own party, cake and ice cream, like the Knicks were the only team in the world. Oh, no!"

Mel was particularly angry because the same year the Knicks triumphed, the Pacers won their first ABA crown and were hardly mentioned in newspapers and sports magazines. The newsmen defended their lopsided coverage, suggesting that the quality of play in the NBA was far above that of the younger league. There may have been some truth to this argument, especially during the ABA's early years. But it hurt when fine players like Daniels were ignored or put down just because they were playing in the ABA. It was a matter of pride.

Daniels was full of pride, and nothing brought it out quicker than having his ability questioned. "I think I can play on a par with centers in the NBA," he stated. "I think I'm just as strong as any of 'em, and I feel I would hold my own against Alcindor [Kareem Abdul-Jabbar] and Chamberlain as well as any other centers in the NBA do.

"The question I keep asking myself is: 'Can they play against me?' That may sound cocky, but they haven't proved a thing to me."

Daniels' negative attitude toward the NBA dated back to 1967. At that time Mel was an All-America, fresh out of the University of New Mexico. He was the first draft pick of the NBA's Cincinnati Royals (now the Kansas City–Omaha Kings).

"When I sat down to talk with Pepper Wilson, who was the Royals' general manager then, I really got sick. They offered me $14,000. I said, 'Is that the bonus?' He said, 'No, that's the salary.' I had to ask him again. I was hurt, shattered, completely destroyed. You have a vision in college that you're pretty good, and I thought being All-America was worth a little more than $14,000."

If he had been drafted just one year earlier, Mel would have had to play for the Royals on their terms or find a new career. But in 1967 the American Basketball Association was getting ready for its opening season. The new league was courting countless college players, hoping that at least a few would bypass the NBA and take a chance with the ABA. But they didn't have much luck. Daniels was the first—and only—big-name college player to sign with the ABA that season. He was drafted by the Minnesota Muskies and got a $29,000 no-cut contract—more than twice the amount he had been offered by the Royals.

The new league looked a little shaky that first fall when Mel headed for Minneapolis to start his pro career. But for Daniels, who had once seemed likely to spend his life working in a car wash or doing time in jail, the ABA was the big time.

Mel grew up in Detroit's black ghetto. His family was very poor, and he saw that the only way out of that poverty was to work or steal. Mel did both. He had a job after school and on weekends, but "I was a thief," he admitted grimly. "Not an out-and-out thief, but I would steal hub-caps, things like that. My parents were good. It was the group I was with. When I was in high school I began looking like a class-A hood, with my hair all plastered down."

Mel went to Pershing High School, which was known for its fine basketball teams. But Daniels had no interest in sports. "I didn't know anything about athletics. I didn't care," he said. In his sophomore year, however, Mel had a sudden change of heart. On his way to class one day he turned a corner and bumped square into Will Robinson, Pershing's basketball coach. Daniels recalled: "Robinson said, 'Son, where have you been? You're going to play basketball.' He gave me a pair of size 14 sneakers, told me to cut my hair and ordered me out to practice the next day. I was pathetic, but Will Robinson kept after me."

Coach Robinson recognized a promising player when he saw one. He changed Daniels from a budding thief into a budding star. And Mel soon discovered that he really did care about athletics. He and coach Robinson worked hard, and their efforts showed. By the end of his senior year Mel was good enough to get scholarship offers from several colleges. He chose the University of New Mexico.

Daniels had a great time at the university with Bob King's Lobos. At Pershing High he had gotten used to the fast break, run-and-shoot type of game. But he quickly adjusted to New Mexico's controlled pattern offense. And Daniels continued to play his steady-scoring, fierce-rebounding style.

During Mel's three varsity seasons, the Lobos enjoyed a 51–24 record. In his senior year they reached the second round of the National Invitational Tournament. The agile center set all kinds of records at the university. While the Lobos were averaging about 65 points a game, Mel had nights of 39 and 34 points—school highs. In three years he

Mel Daniels: from budding thief to budding star.

set a scoring record of 1,537 points (19.7 per game) and a rebounding record of 854 total caroms (11 per game).

But one of the most memorable moments in Daniels' college career doesn't even appear in the record book. In Mel's junior year (1965–66) New Mexico was playing Utah. Daniels was having a typically good match. At half time the teams broke play and headed for their lockers. The door to the Lobos' locker room had a plate-glass window. When Mel pushed the entrance bar, his hand slipped and his left arm went through the glass. He fell forward, slicing his arm and face on the jagged glass.

The wound was serious, very serious. Mel's arm was cut open to the bone, and 250 stitches were required to close it. Luckily, he had missed severing a vital nerve by just half an inch. If that nerve had been damaged, Daniels would have permanently lost the use of his left arm.

Daniels stubbornly refused to be stopped by the injury. He missed only one game, covering his arm with foam padding to play the remaining ten matches on the schedule. Between games he worked with weights to get the arm back in shape. He finished his junior year with an amazing 21.2-point average and over ten rebounds a game. He was named all-conference.

Statistically, Mel's senior year was even better.

He averaged 21.5 points and 11.6 rebounds and was named to many All-America teams.

The following year Mel went from New Mexico to the ABA's Minnesota team and from All-America to All-Star. The young rookie got off to such a great start with the Muskies that he was named to the East squad for the ABA's first All-Star game in 1968. Held at Indianapolis' Hinkel Field House, the match provided Mel with an opportunity to show off his talents.

The East led during most of the game, but by very narrow margins. In the last twelve minutes of play Larry Brown, a small, lightning-quick guard, came off the West bench to spark his team ahead with nine points in five minutes. When Brown left the game there were seven minutes on the clock and the West was out in front, 108–104. But the remaining time belonged to the East—and Mel Daniels. He took complete control of the game, scoring and rebounding at will. With three minutes to go, he muscled in for a lay-up that gave the East a two-point lead. The East finally won, 126–120.

By the end of the 1967–68 season he was the runaway choice for the Rookie of the Year award. He had averaged 22.2 points and 15.5 rebounds a game. In addition, he had a total of 1,213 rebounds, the highest in the league.

After his great rookie season with Minnesota, Daniels was traded to the Indiana Pacers. The

Muskies hated to lose him, of course, but the club was an economic failure and needed a lot of money to pay its bills. The Pacers put up $100,000 and two lesser players for their new center.

That deal may rank with the Louisiana Purchase as one of the great steals of all time. The Muskies paid their debts, later moved to Miami and finally folded altogether. The Pacers—with Mel in the pivot—became the best organized, most stable team in the league.

In his first season with Indiana (1968–69), Mel really showed what he could do. He led the team in scoring (24 points per game) and rebounds (16.2 per game, the highest in the ABA). By the end of the season he had established himself as the ABA's best big man and been named the league's Most Valuable Player.

In 1970–71, Daniels was again the league's MVP. On the way to that honor he snagged his 5,000th rebound, making him the top ABA man in that department. He led the league in rebounds (averaging 17.9 a game) and the Pacers in scoring (21 points a game). He also got 29 points and 13 rebounds in the 1971 All-Star game to grab MVP honors there.

Yet Mel's appearance belied his great strength. Compared to Kareem Abdul-Jabbar or Wilt Chamberlain—the NBA centers he most respected —Mel was downright skinny. He was 6-foot-9 and

Daniels (#34) goes up for a rebound in the 1969 ABA All-Star game.

weighed in at a mere 225. But during a game he was the most dominating force on the court. Smart opponents steered clear of him. Others, less cautious, drove in only to have their shots slammed back into their faces or get hit by one of Mel's sharp elbows in a rebounding duel.

"He keeps improving and improving and improving," marveled Indiana's coach, Bob Leonard. "And the reason is because he's a competitor, a winner. When he isn't playing good offense, he's playing good defense. And when he isn't playing good defense, he's playing good offense. And when he isn't playing good offense or defense, he's rebounding. Mel mixes the three together as much as you possibly can."

Mel was always in perpetual motion, even during the offseason. When he wasn't writing poetry he was busy riding horseback or teaching youngsters basketball skills.

When I was a junior at New Mexico," he recalled, "I asked Ira Harge [a Lobo teammate, who later went on to play with the Utah Stars] to take me to a stable. I had always loved horses and I wanted to ride. Since then, I've spent thousands of hours in a saddle. In school I used to ride up into the hills or just alongside the Rio Grande."

Daniels and his partner, Pacer teammate Roger Brown, owned several horses at a stable outside Indianapolis. But Daniels did the bulk of his riding in

New Mexico, where he had his offseason home. On any given day in the late spring or summer months, he could be found guiding a horse over the rugged southwestern landscape or inside some Albuquerque gym guiding the athletic fortunes of a group of poor youngsters. His youth work was very important to Mel. "I try to teach my team of eleven- to sixteen-year-olds the same things Will Robinson taught me," he explained.

If Mel had any free time after all that, he could probably use it up polishing the pile of trophies, plaques and awards he earned in the ABA. But all the titles and pats on the back didn't mean anything as long as there were people who still considered the ABA a bush league. So Daniels always gave a little extra whenever he went against NBA players in exhibition games. It paid off, too. Win or lose, he never failed to get praise from the other league's men. Mel hoped a day would come when that praise could be an everyday occurence. History was on his side.

"Look at Len Dawson," he pointed out. "They kind of snubbed him in the National Football League. Then he got a chance to prove himself in the American Football League and ended up winning the Super Bowl. Len Dawson was a mind-changer, and that's what we're going to have to have. I personally think we've got 'em in the ABA, if we only have a merger to show it."

2.

Bob Love

When Bob Love was a youngster he practiced basketball by tossing a stuffed sock through a rusty barrel rim nailed to a tree. He lived in Bastrop, Louisiana, a rural black community, which lacked the concrete courts so common in the big cities of the North. Love spent many afternoons with his makeshift equipment, never realizing that one day he would be one of the great forwards in the NBA.

"Forwards like Connie Hawkins and Billy Cunningham get all the write-ups," said the 6-foot-8 Love, "but they're no tougher than I am. They need the ball to score, and I can score without it."

Bob Love drives for a shot against the Celtics.

That may sound like incredible bragging, but on many occasions Bob did get the best of a Hawkins or a Cunningham. And if he couldn't actually score without the ball, he could certainly do the next best thing. Love's rivals were often the fabulous one-on-one artists—men who specialized in getting the ball, beating the defender with their spectacular moves and then scoring. But Bob didn't need the ball to work his brand of magic. He was always in motion, dancing and darting around the floor, looking to shake free of the man guarding him. He got open first, *then* he got the ball and scored!

"Maybe I'll have to use my head more and my legs less when I get older," he admitted, "but I don't get tired anyway. I move a lot, although I've learned to do it at the right time. Other guys work harder with a lot of wasted effort.

"Those one-on-one players get tired dribbling, and they have somebody knocking them down all the time. I don't get a lot of contact because I use finesse, not muscle."

"Poor boy makes good in the NBA" is a common story, especially among the league's black ballplayers. But Bob Love's story was more than that. When he joined the pro circuit in 1965, Love was no rookie star. Although he played well in exhibitions and worked hard in practice, no one seemed to notice him. He spent his first three years in the NBA on the benches of three different teams.

For a long time it seemed that there would be no happy ending for Bob. How he finally got into a starting line-up and made believers out of doubters is a tale of a "Cinderella" player whose pride and confidence finally paid off.

It's hard to imagine where Bob got his confidence. Certainly there was little in his childhood to cause anything but frustration. His mother worked as a maid for $12 a week to feed her family. Food was scarce around the Love household. The family ate best on Sundays, and Bob said the daily menu was most often "chicken necks, chicken guts and chicken feet."

Love worked from the time he was old enough to walk. He picked cotton and baled hay under the burning Louisiana sun. The only clothes he wore were hand-me-downs, and the very first suit he bought was for his high school graduation.

It's easy to see where a youngster could get the itch to escape that kind of life. With Bob, it was more than an itch—it was an obsession. "As a kid, I was pretty big and fast. For people like us, the only way out you ever heard about was sports. By the time I was a sophomore in high school, I knew I was going to be a pro athlete—that I had to be. At that time I didn't know in which sport."

Love was quite a football player in high school. His passing arm was so good that he earned all-

Bob Love: a "Cinderella" story.

state quarterback honors three years in a row. He knew he wouldn't have any trouble getting a college scholarship in the sport. The question was: at what position? Bob was lanky, tall and quick—an ideal end. He was afraid some college coach would want him to catch the ball instead of throw it.

And then there was basketball. Bob first began playing the game during lunchtime breaks in high school. The stars of those pickup games were the players from the school basketball team. At first Love was no match for them, and that bothered him. He didn't like being shown up. So whenever he had some free time after school and work, he would practice alone with his stuffed sock and barrel hoop. The results were almost immediate. Soon it was the basketball team members who were being shown up in the lunchtime battles.

"I used to score on them like they were nothing," he proudly recalled. "They told the coach about me and one day he told me, 'You stop playing against them and get with them.' So I went out for the team, and I was sixth man in my junior year. My last year I started, and I've been playing ever since—though not always starting."

Love went from Bastrop's Morehouse High to Southern University in Baton Rouge on full scholarship. Playing center, he led the Jaguar freshmen to a 26–2 record. Switching between forward and center for the next three years, Bob averaged 25 points a game and took the team into the NAIA (small college) semi-finals his senior year. He had an excellent reputation for his movement both on offense and defense.

Bob had an unusual explanation for his success: "A stuffed sock doesn't bounce too well, so all I could do was 'air dribble,' which means you take the sock by the loose end and pretend you're bouncing a basketball. A lot of people think I learned my running, moving-without-the-ball game in college. But that's the *only* way when you learn your basketball using a sock."

The year Love graduated, 1965, was a big one for college talent. It was the year the NBA drafted Billy Cunningham, the Van Arsdale brothers, Dave Stallworth, Bill Bradley, Gail Goodrich, Flynn Robinson and Keith Erickson. All those players were picked on the first and second rounds of the draft. Love went to the Cincinnati Royals on the fourth round. He expected to go higher but, as he soon discovered, basketball stars from all-black colleges were not as highly regarded by the pros as football standouts from the same institutions.

Bob's fine college statistics counted for little with the Royals because he wasn't a "name" player. They offered him $9,000 to sign, and he took it. There was nothing else he could do. He couldn't threaten to sign with a team in the American Basketball Association because the ABA had not even been formed at the time. Although Bob was grateful for the chance to prove himself in the big league, his pride was hurt. Then the Royals added insult to injury by farming him out to a team in the Eastern League (basketball's "minors") before he even had a chance to prove what he could do.

Bob responded by averaging 24 points and 18 rebounds a game in the 1965–66 season. But that was in the minors. Cincinnati rewarded his fine performance there by giving him a seat on their bench the next season. The Royals had Jerry

Lucas, Happy Hairston and John Tresvant playing forward, so Bob got very little playing time. As a spot player, he averaged 6.7 points per game his first year in the NBA.

Looking back on that year, only two events stood out in Bob's mind: he injured his back near the end of the year, and he was chosen by Oscar Robertson for a roommate. "I think he was intrigued by my nickname," Love chuckled. Bob was called "Butterbean," a name he picked up in high school because he loved the vegetable.

The 1967–68 season wasn't any more memorable. When someone was needed to give a deliberate foul, Bob sometimes got a little time on the court. But more often than not, he sat on the sidelines and waited. Not surprisingly, his season's average was a mere 6.4 points.

His big chance seemed to come at the end of the year, when he was sent to Milwaukee in the expansion draft. For a time, Love was happy. "I was glad to get away from the Royals. Whenever I played with Cincinnati, I was playing with Oscar," he explained, implying that Robertson left few opportunities for anyone else to score. "And they only put me in against teams like the Lakers, when I'd have to go against West or Baylor. I was glad to go to Milwaukee, 'cause here was a chance to get playing time and show what I could do."

Bob did show that he could excel. During the

exhibition season he led the Bucks in scoring, with 17 points a game. But when the regular season began, it was the same old nightmare. Love was watching the action from the bench.

Then, once again, he seemed to get another chance, another hope. The Bucks traded Love and guard Bob Weiss to the Chicago Bulls for guard Flynn Robinson. Bob had hardly gotten his seat warm in Milwaukee when suddenly he was off to another city.

Bob joined the Bulls in November 1968, much to the displeasure of the Chicago fans. The first time he made an appearance in a Chicago uniform, he was booed unmercifully. It wasn't his fault. Unfortunately, he already had the reputation of being a marginal player—a guy who might hang on in the league another couple of years, if he was lucky. The man Chicago had given up for Love was Flynn Robinson, a local favorite. As a Bull, Robinson had been a pure shooter, a gunner. He could bring a crowd to its feet with his long, arcing jump shots. But while the fans thought he was the greatest, the coaches were much less enthusiastic. The trouble was, when Robinson had the ball, the rest of the Bulls just stood around with nothing to do. In addition, Robinson's defensive play wasn't very good.

As a Milwaukee rookie in 1968, Bob makes the most of one of his rare appearances on the court.

The story goes that Chicago coach Dick Motta, a very emotional man, decided Robinson had to go. He wanted team play from the Bulls, and Robinson's style seemed to produce an "everyone for himself" attitude. One day Motta called up Dick Klein, who was then the Bulls' general manager, and issued an ultimatum. "If Robinson shows up at the stadium," the coach threatened, "I won't be there."

Still, Robinson had been one of the few players on the roster that the Chicago fans could cheer. Naturally, they booed his replacement, a man earmarked second-rate ever since he came into the NBA. It didn't help matters, either, when Love reinjured his back in an auto accident soon after joining Chicago. The 1968–69 season was a total failure for Love. He appeared in 49 games and averaged just 5.9 points. Three years in the NBA and his scoring had gone down steadily.

"Bob never said one complaining word to me while he was sitting on the bench," Motta said.

Love never said one complaining word to any of his NBA coaches, and perhaps it wasn't only pride that sealed his lips. More likely it was his speech handicap that made it difficult for Bob to speak up to a coach. Bob had always had a bad stutter. It didn't prevent him from calling signals on the football field or being popular with his buddies or doing his work in college or finding a girl to marry. But he couldn't seem to walk up to his bosses and tell them why he should be playing. He might get too nervous, and the nervousness would make him stutter more.

Some coaches may have gotten the wrong idea. Perhaps they thought that because he silently accepted his spot on the bench, Love lacked confidence or simply didn't care whether he played or not.

The Bulls were looking for change in the 1969–70 season, but they weren't looking to Love. In their attempts to strengthen their frontcourt, they ignored the eager young man. Before the start of the campaign, they traded Jim Washington to Philadelphia for veteran Chet Walker. It was a fine deal. But the one that followed it was not so fine. Searching for a forward to team with Walker, the name Bob Kauffman of Seattle came up. As Motta put it, "One of my scouts fell in love with Kauffman for his strength off the boards. I hadn't seen him play that much, but we took the scout's word that he could do the job."

For Kauffman, the SuperSonics wanted two forwards—Bob Boozer and a throw-in. Chicago offered to throw in Bob Love. Nothing doing, said the Seattle management. Who's Bob Love? A nobody, a nothing. Seattle wanted Bull forward Barry Clemens instead, and they got him.

Walker and Kauffman started the season as the Bulls' forwards. On paper it looked great, but in reality it didn't work out. Walker was everything Chi-

cago had hoped for, but Kauffman tended to slow
down the offense. The Bulls kept falling behind
early in their games, and only last-minute heroics
were saving them. The hero? Who else but Bob
Love!

In one early-season match against the Lakers,
Love came off the bench with his team far behind.
The Lakers eventually won by four points—but not
before Bob scored 23 points and sparked the rest of
his teammates in a fourth quarter rally. A couple of
nights later, he replaced Kauffman and was largely
responsible for a two-point victory over the Sonics,
the team that hadn't wanted him. Love then went
on to score 34 points in a win against the Warriors.
And another time he scored 34 points in a 152–123
triumph over the Suns—and one of the toughest
frontcourts in the league.

Suddenly people were talking about Bob Love.
Suddenly the fans were cheering him. Suddenly,
the Chicago management fell out of love with Bob
Kauffman, and Bob Love took over the starting
spot. He was ready for it, mentally and physically.
He had kept himself in shape during the offseason.
"I always wanted to be sure that if my chance came
I would be in good enough shape to take advantage
of it," Love said. "And I always said that if I ever
got into the line-up, nobody would ever get me out
of it."

Of course, nobody even tried. Love and Walker

Everyone in Chicago loves Love. Here the Bulls' forward is one-on-one against another big man—Laker Jerry West.

made a perfect duo up front. Walker was a good outside shooter and rebounder. He was also the one who matched muscle with the big boys under the hoop. Bob, admittedly no rebounder, was free to move as he chose. One observer wrote that Love "picks up about ten points a game by slipping free underneath to take a quick pass for the unmolested basket."

Bob averaged 21 points a game in the 1969–70 season and was named to the NBA All-Star West squad. The midseason contest was particularly important to Love. "Everyone else, or almost everybody, was an established pro, a household name," he explained. "They were there to have some fun and for the honor of it. I was there for the honor of it, too, but I was going to have to earn it down the court."

Love might have seemed a bit out of place in the 1970 All-Star game, among men like West, Robertson, Alcindor (Kareem Abdul-Jabbar) and Chamberlain. But when the half-time statistics were tallied, it was Bob Love who led all the scorers (with 13 points). One TV announcer seemed so amazed to find an unknown holding that place of esteem that he almost choked reading the news. Overall, Bob finished third in the game's scoring, and he did it before a national audience. He was truly a star.

"I hear people talking about me, calling me a surprise," he said. "What I'm doing is no surprise to me. I always could shoot, score and play defense. You can have all the potential in the world, but it doesn't help if you're sitting on the bench."

The Bulls reached the playoffs at the end of

1970, but lost to Atlanta in four games. Both Love and the team improved in 1970–71. Once again he led the team in scoring, with a 25.2-point average, and Chicago went on to its best record ever, 51–31. The Bulls finished second, behind Milwaukee, in the rugged Midwest Division and went into the playoffs against Los Angeles.

It took seven games for the Lakers to beat them, and what a contest it was! Only two of the games were decided by margins of more than ten points. Love averaged 26.7 points in the seven battles. He used his slender 215-pound frame to keep hot-scoring rookie Jim McMillian away from the basketball—a superb defensive performance. On offense, he was even more fantastic. In the third game, for example, he scored 27 points (17 in the fourth quarter) to rally Chicago to a 106–98 victory. In the following game he rammed home 36 points, and the Bulls won, 112–102.

Bob continued his fine play in 1971–72. Again he made the All-Star West team—but this time everyone knew his name. His statistics reflected his growing talents. He finished sixth in league scoring with 25.8 points per game and averaged 18.8 points in the Bulls' four postseason games.

"It's more fun now," he said at the end of that season. "I can do things on the floor when the opportunity comes up. I have more confidence in myself, and I can see I'm getting more respect."

From that time on, the league's best defensive players were sent in to guard Bob. The sportwriters still tended to look past him, but the players didn't. For he had finally found his place among the college stars of 1965—the ones who went ahead of him in the draft.

How did he do it? What was Bob Love's success formula? Bob had a simple answer: "I knew I could play—that's all there is to it. A lot of guys get a few bad breaks and quit. Some kind of inner pride kept me going, because I was convinced I could play as well as anyone in the league."

3.

Dan Issel

Some pro basketball players become all-stars at center. Others get their recognition playing forward. But rarely does a man shine at both positions. Dan Issel was one of the few who did. As a rookie center with the ABA's Kentucky Colonels in 1970–71, Issel led the league in scoring. In his second pro year Dan switched to forward and again enjoyed all-league status.

It wasn't as easy as Dan made it look, though. The two positions demand different skills. To excel at both spots he needed muscle, good hands, quickness and the ability to shoot accurately near or far from the basket. It often takes years for a player to master a new position, but Issel did it in just one.

Before Dan moved to forward a reporter asked

coach Frank Ramsey if he expected Issel to have difficulty with the change. Ramsey, who had coached Dan his rookie season, seemed sure there would be no problem. "Dan is quicker than most centers," he explained. "He has a very fast first step, and if you play him tight he'll take that quick step and he's gone. Dan scored a lot of points driving by his opponents.

"It's determination," Ramsey continued. "I respect him more for that than anything else. Determination made Dan a fine center, and it will probably make him one of basketball's best forwards."

Determination played an important part in Dan's life. Naturally, all successful athletes make it through determined effort. For most great sports figures, it's a matter of combining determination with obvious talent. But in Issel's case it was a different story. Dan had the drive all right—but for years the talent was far from obvious.

Dan grew up in the basketball-mad Midwest. Born in Geneva, Illinois, in 1948, he moved with his family to Sedalia, Missouri, and finally settled in Batavia, Illinois, at age twelve. Like his schoolmates, he played football, baseball and basketball and ran track, although he wasn't much good at any of them. Part of the problem was that sports were not really important to him. Dan was an excellent student, and much of his attention went to his studies.

Dan Issel: determination was the key.

Batavia High School had a rather poor basketball team, so it was no great accomplishment when Dan won a place on the bench. At that time he was six feet tall—a definite plus for a young high school player. He even got to start a few games his freshman year when the regular starter broke a leg. But basically, Issel was just another big, awkward youth on the court. He certainly didn't play like a future pro star. In fact, he didn't even play like a future high school star.

Dan might have given up basketball and gone on to become a doctor or a lawyer. But two dramatic changes occurred after his sophomore year in high school. That summer Batavia hired a new basketball coach—and Dan shot up to an awesome 6-foot-7. The new coach, Donovan Vandersnick, knew his job. He had previously coached several teams at Galva, Illinois, into state tournaments.

Vandersnick got right down to work. Under his outstanding coaching the boys made incredible progress. By the time Batavia took the court in 1963 it looked like a different team—physically strong and confident of winning. And strange as it seems, the focal point of this new group was Dan Issel. Vandersnick had taken a special interest in Issel, seeing a potential in the youngster that others had missed. Long hours of grueling practice began to pay off, and Dan's talents became more apparent every day.

That year Batavia lost only two of its 30 games in the regular season and shocked everyone (except their coach, of course) by going on to the state sectional tourney. Issel was named to the all-conference team, and college scouts began to contact him.

No one was more surprised at the attention

Issel received than Dan himself. A modest man, he was critical of his own play. "As a junior," he recalled years later, "I was a clumsy sophomore."

If the praise of others did nothing else, however, it made Dan realize how much he enjoyed the sport. "I decided I wanted to play basketball more than anything else," he said. "There was also the prestige. People who excelled in athletics were looked up to."

In his senior year Dan again led Batavia into the sectionals. Many more people took notice of the tall, blond scorer. Issel made the all-state squad, and scholarship offers poured in. The Big Ten Conference schools were particularly eager to get Issel, and for a while it looked as if he would go to one of them.

"I liked Wisconsin best," he explained, "but my parents were impressed with the academic standing of Northwestern and wanted me to go there. I signed a letter of intent, but I wasn't too hot on Northwestern. A friend of mine who went there told me there was a lot of money at Northwestern —that the girls wore mink coats to fraternity parties. I didn't think a farm boy from Batavia was ready for that."

But Dan *was* ready to play basketball, and there were few better places to play it than the University of Kentucky. Issel's dad suggested the school, and it was a perfect choice. Kentucky was the perennial

Dan was the man at the University of Kentucky.

champion of the Southeastern Conference and one of college basketball's super-powers. Under coach Adolf Rupp, players like Cliff Hagan, Alex Groza and Cotton Nash had soared to All-America status and eventual professional stardom.

Kentucky attracted some of the top high school cagers in the nation, so Dan's glowing newspaper clippings didn't mean much there. He did receive a full scholarship from the university. But although his presence was welcome, it wasn't really big news. "I'll never forget my first visit to Lexington [home of the university]," he said with a grin. "I picked up a newspaper and read that Rupp's first choice for his center of the future was somebody from Iowa—his name escapes me now—and that his second choice was George Janky. I wasn't even mentioned."

Perhaps Dan wasn't mentioned because coach Rupp, a fine judge of talent, felt Issel had a lot to learn. Still, the fact remains that Dan did start every game for the Kentucky Wildcats. He wasn't an instant success. In fact, in one game early in his sophomore year Issel played 25 minutes, took just two shots—missing both—and pulled down only two rebounds.

Dan knew he could do better than that. Fortunately, so did Adolf Rupp. The coach let him keep trying, and with each game, the young center improved. His shots began to find their target, and he became more aggressive off the boards. At the end of his sophomore season he had averaged 16.4 points and more than 12 rebounds per game.

The rest is history—Kentucky basketball history. Issel's scoring average jumped to 26.6 points per game in his junior year and 33.9 (fourth best in the nation) his senior year. He broke many of the Wildcats' long-standing records, accumulating

2,138 points and a 25.7 points-per-game average over a three-year varsity career as well as 53 points in a single game. He was an All-America twice.

But statistics can't tell the whole story of Dan's magnificent career at Kentucky. He also had a very special relationship with his coach. Adolf Rupp was not an easy man to get along with. Nicknamed "the Baron" for his domineering ways, Rupp was one of college basketball's oldest and most success- ful coaches. He was a very demanding man— tough, abrasive, dedicated and very much set in his ways.

After watching Kentucky in a pregame work- out, one sportswriter wrote about the players' ap- pearance. "There was nary a hint of a sideburn, mustache or beard, and they all looked as though their last act before leaving the locker room was to scrub their faces thoroughly."

The Kentucky players were only meeting coach Rupp's stern requirements. According to his rules, they couldn't wear long hair, or drink, or stay out late or even get married. While Issel was on the team, however, four players defied Rupp and got married during one season. One of those players was Dan Issel, and though Rupp grumbled about kicking the whole bunch off the team, he couldn't bring himself to discipline them. Especially Dan. He liked the boy too much.

During his senior year Issel was asked how he avoided getting into any serious scrapes with the

Baron. "It wasn't that difficult," he answered. "My high school coach was real strict, too, and ran basically the same offense. I learned that you have to take coach Rupp's criticism constructively. He wants everything perfect. I certainly respect him. He stresses teamwork, and I'm as surprised as anyone that I scored so much here. This is far from a one-man team."

The same determination that had made Dan a high school star helped make him a college superstar. For example, during a game against the Tennessee Volunteers in his senior year Dan was moved to forward in an attempt to crack the tough Tennessee zone defense. Playing the unfamiliar position, however, wasn't Issel's only problem. He had the flu and was both feverish and dizzy. Tennessee was freezing the ball, but by half time Kentucky had a slim 26–23 lead. Issel hadn't gotten his hands on the ball often enough to be much of a scoring factor, but he had managed to block three Tennessee shots and make two steals.

The Volunteers continued to freeze the ball in the second half. College basketball had no shooting clock, so they could dribble around as much as they liked. Whenever the Wildcat defense relaxed, Tennessee tried to get the ball to their 6-foot-10 All-America center, Bobby Croft. But Kentucky continued to steal the ball and began to lengthen its lead.

The turning point in the match came when Issel

snatched a rebound and banked in an eight-foot jumper. In desperation, Croft had fouled his smaller opponent on the shot. Dan made his free throw, and Croft went to the bench. With their big man in foul trouble, the Vols fell apart. Dan led Kentucky fast breaks, grabbed rebounds at both ends of the court and harrassed Tennessee unmercifully on defense. When the game ended, Kentucky was in front, 68–52. Issel had 28 points and 11 rebounds. "I didn't know where he was most of the time," Croft muttered after the match.

The Volunteer center may not have known where to find Dan, but the pro scouts did. Issel left the University of Kentucky in 1970, at the very height of the power struggle between the NBA and the ABA for new players. The NBA wanted Issel badly. Red Auerbach, general manager and former coach of the Boston Celtics, summed up his league's judgment of the Kentucky center: "You figure the kid's going to be a hell of a pro cornerman, but then again he's strong enough to play center. He shoots well, he's quick, he comes down with the ball—what more can you ask?"

It was a great year for young talent. Charlie Scott, Calvin Murphy, Pete Maravich, Bob Lanier and Jim McMillian were only a few of the big-name college players to enter the pro leagues that season. So the NBA was sure to get its share of outstanding rookies no matter where Issel went.

But for the ABA it was another matter—a matter of survival. Only one year before, the leagues had engaged in a vicious bidding war over Lew Alcindor (Kareem Abdul-Jabbar). The ABA was suffering from a lack of nationally known stars. They needed Alcindor to boost game attendance, and keep the weaker teams from going broke. It was a big loss for the young league when Alcindor eventually signed with the NBA's Milwaukee team.

So 1970 was a crucial year for the ABA. And it was especially crucial for the Kentucky Colonels. A money-losing club, the Colonels had just changed ownership. The first thing Kentucky's new president, Wendell Cherry, and general manager, Mike Storen, wanted to do was sign the boy from Batavia. "If we do anything," Cherry told the press, "we're going to get Dan Issel."

Of course, Issel was a natural selection. He was not only famous throughout the land, he was practically a hometown hero in Kentucky. Dan was just the player to fill Freedom Hall, the Colonels' home court, with fans.

"After you're down here for a while," Dan said just before negotiations began, "you can't help but think of yourself as a Kentuckian. Everyone goes out of his way to make you feel at home. I know this will be the Colonels' big pitch to me—to keep playing before the same people who cheered me in college. But I'm keeping my options open. I guess I

As a Kentucky Colonel, Issel shoots against the Virginia Squires.

have some obligation to Kentucky, but I have a greater obligation to my own and my wife's future. If you want to put it this way: 'Money talks.'"

The Colonels' money spoke loud and clear—in the neighborhood of 1.4 million dollars! That was the kind of money Milwaukee had given to Lew Alcindor. When Dan signed the Kentucky contract, he said: "I know more people are waiting for me to flop than succeed. To people who have to report to an assembly line every day, that's too much money for a guy playing a game. But I put the pressure on myself. I wanted it. It would have been a lot easier to go out drinking than to go to basketball practice at the university. Because some players are getting a lot of money nowadays, well, we shouldn't get condemned for that. That's the situation with the NBA and ABA fighting. I worked, and I worked hard, to get here. I've had to prove myself everywhere, and I still have to prove myself with the Colonels."

And Issel did prove himself. Soon after Dan arrived at his first pro camp, the Colonels traded away their veteran center, Gene Moore. Issel was immediately thrust into the pivot spot. "Mel Daniels will murder Dan at first," predicted general manager Storen. "But after four or five games, Daniels won't look as fierce to Dan. But that first time—oh, it's going to be murder!"

Daniels, the Indiana Pacers' All-Star center, did humble his rookie opponent in their first two contests. But the third time they met it was Issel who was in control. He outscored Daniels 27 points to 18, and outrebounded him 20 to 11.

Issel had what it takes to be a fine center. At 6-foot-9 and 240 pounds, he wasn't especially big for a pivotman, but he certainly was strong. No other

ABA center could push him around once he'd learned the ropes. And Issel—who had expected to play forward—had the mobility of a cornerman. He was just as effective shooting 15 and 20 feet away from the hoop as he was close in.

At midyear Issel scored 21 points in the ABA All-Star game. And by the end of the 1970–71 season Dan led the ABA in scoring with an average of 29.1 points per game. He also brought down over 13 rebounds a game. His great performances earned him co-Rookie of the Year honors with Virginia's Charlie Scott.

Dan's only disappointment in 1970–71 came in the playoffs. Kentucky went all the way to the final round, then lost the championship to the Utah Stars in seven games, Issel was the second highest scorer in the playoffs, averaging 28.1 points in 19 games.

All in all, it was a tremendous season. Issel had made the Colonels winners. He had given the ABA a player of national stature. And he had boosted Kentucky's attendance by 46 percent.

In Dan's second pro season Kentucky signed Artis Gilmore, a 7-foot-2 giant from Jacksonville, to play pivot and moved Issel to forward. Dan actually felt more at home in his new spot. "Playing forward," he said, "it's a lot easier to get the ball. There are picks and screens and usually they don't double-team a forward. It's pretty hard for a team

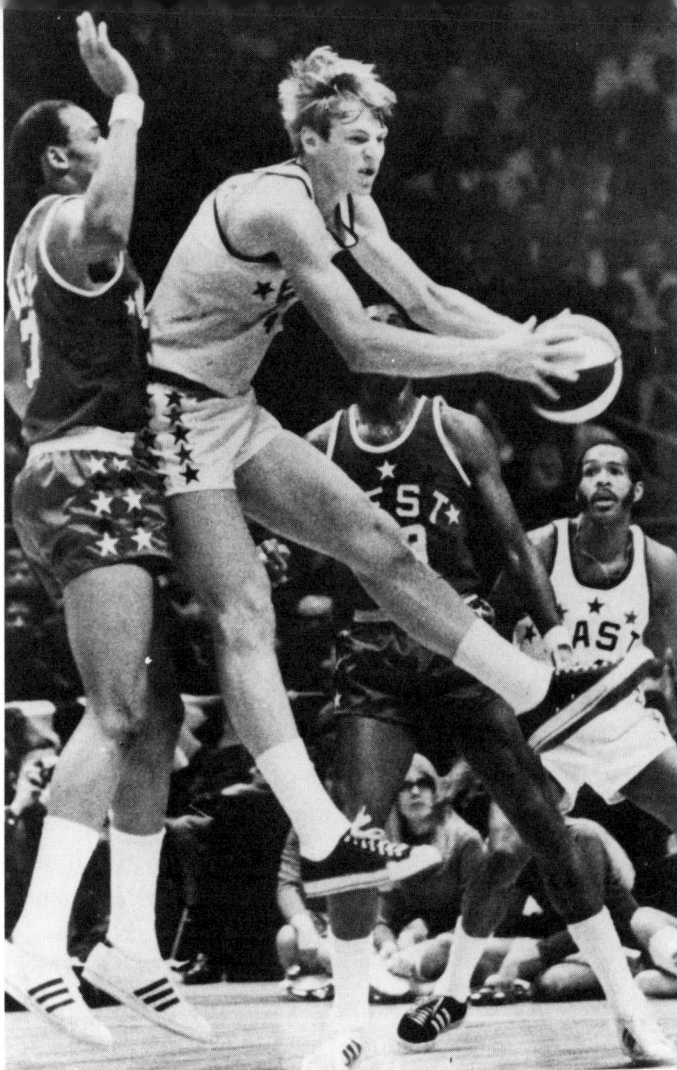

Issel slams into Zelmo Beaty during the 1971 ABA All-Star game.

to fall off on you, because they're leaving someone else closer to the basket open. At center, I had to work myself open. It's a lot easier for a team to slough-off, double-team, on the man in the middle.

Now, I'm not so closely guarded, so I'm getting more shots."

In 1971–72 the Colonels finished the regular season with a 68–16 record (the best in ABA history), and most observers expected them to win the championship. But again the Colonels were disappointed. They were defeated by the Nets in the first playoff round. Issel was held to a 22-point average in six matches.

But one defeat couldn't take away a whole year of achievement. Dan ranked third in the league in regular season scoring with 30.5 points per game and pulled down 11 rebounds per game. In addition, Issel scored a league-leading total of 2,538 points for the year.

A great showcase for Dan's many talents was the 1971 All-Star game. The contest started with balance and teamwork on both sides but finally turned into a one-on-one shoot-out. Issel finished the game with 21 points, nine rebounds and five assists in 24 minutes of play. Jim McDaniels wound up with more points, and New York's Rick Barry grabbed more rebounds. But Dan Issel walked off with Most Valuable Player honors for his willingness—and great ability—to play a team game.

"Look," said Dan's coach, Joe Mullaney, "good game or bad game, I know he's giving everything he's got out there, and that he'll get the job done."

What more can you say of any player?

4.

Hal Greer

Hal Greer has been called "the most obscure 20,000-point scorer in the history of professional basketball," and that was a pretty good way to describe the NBA's Grand Old Man. Greer was only the sixth man to reach the 20,000-point scoring mark, and no one had appeared in more NBA games. The name "Hal Greer" was printed all over the record books: he ranked in the top ten in career assists, field goals attempted and made, playing time and even (on the negative side) personal fouls.

But in his many years as a guard with the Syracuse Nationals (later known as the Philadelphia 76ers) Hal's game-by-game achievements were often overshadowed by those of his more famous

teammates. He played alongside such superstars as Dolph Schayes, Wilt Chamberlain and Billy Cunningham, men who didn't leave much room on the sports pages for anyone else. So Hal had to fight for recognition as well as for points.

And even when his own teammates weren't in the limelight, his opponents were. Take the night Greer tossed in his 20,000th career point. It was January 29, 1971, and the 76ers were playing the flashy Milwaukee Bucks. Hal needed just 20 more points to reach his milestone, and by half time it seemed a cinch. Although Milwaukee was leading, the Sixers only trailed by three and Greer already had 13 points. But in the third quarter the Bucks—with Lew Alcindor (now Kareem Abdul-Jabbar), Oscar Robertson and Bob Dandridge—began to steal the show. They put on a spectacular display, making 60 percent of their shots from the field and holding the 76ers down with a crushing defense.

Greer seemed to tighten up. One of his shots fell a full two feet short of the basket. The Bucks rebounded and scored on a fast break. Hal took another shot, and again it was short. Robertson scored two points from the free-throw line after Hal fouled him on the fast break. By the end of the third quarter Greer had 19 points, but the Bucks

Hal Greer (#15), Bob Dandridge (#10) and Kareem Abdul-Jabbar wait for Greer's 20,000th career point to become official.

had a 91–74 lead. Philadelphia coach Jack Ramsay pulled Greer out of the game for a rest.

In the fourth quarter Hal watched his team fall even farther behind. Sitting on the bench, he even began to doubt he would get his final point that evening. The fans in the Philadelphia Spectrum—including a large number of Hal's friends and relatives—also began to worry. Finally, he went back in the game, only to tangle with Alcindor over a loose ball. Greer, just 6-foot-2, found himself facing the 7-foot-5 center in a jump-ball situation. Hal lost the match-up, of course, but he soon got even.

Greer took a pass and drove toward the basket, which was being guarded by Alcindor. The big man saw Greer coming and moved into position to block Hal's favorite shot, the 15-foot jumper. But instead of pulling up and shooting, Greer drove at the giant. He pushed himself past Alcindor with an extra burst of speed, popping the ball up as his momentum carried him under the backboard. The 15,000 fans stood up and cheered. Thunderous applause filled the arena. Hal Greer had joined Wilt Chamberlain, Elgin Baylor, Bob Pettit, Oscar Robertson and Jerry West in the exclusive 20,000-point club.

That night was the high spot in a long, full career. But basketball was always Hal Greer's world. "I can't remember not having a basketball in my hands," he once told a reporter.

Hal grew up with six brothers and two sisters in Huntington, West Virginia. His father worked for the Chesapeake & Ohio Railroad. The Greers weren't rich, but they weren't poor, either. There was plenty of food on the table and the boys grew up strong and tough. Basketball was their game. Hal recalls playing the sport "all year round, day and night—every day, every night. We had baskets on the back of the doors in every bedroom in the house, including my father's bedroom."

Hal played one-on-one games with his brothers on those bedroom courts. One after another, the Greer boys became heroes in the schoolyard contests and stars at Douglass High School. For a time, J. D. Greer stood out as the best athlete in the family. He was six years older than Hal and a lot bigger.

"J.D. was the greatest high school basketball player I've ever seen," said Greer. "He was the first guy I ever saw guide a shot in the basket—I mean like Dippy [Wilt Chamberlain]. It fascinated me. J.D. was my idol, but he wouldn't let me play with him in the playground games. Soon as I'd show up at the playground, J.D. would yell, 'Get out of here, kid, you want to get hurt?'

"Even after I started playing ball in high school, J.D. always put me down. He used to say, 'I am the greatest in the Greer family.' I guess that's why I have such a strong desire to excel—because I've always wanted to convince J.D. that I was pretty good myself."

"You mustn't forget," explained J.D., "Hal is my kid brother and he'll always be my kid brother. Why, I remember when that little boy went out for basketball at Douglass High. The coach took one look at him and said, 'Son, go home and eat some more beans.'

"I was always looking after him. I wouldn't let him play in those big boy games at the playground because he weighed only about 90 pounds and I was around 200. I was afraid he might get hurt. I didn't think a little boy like that could take the punches we handed out."

But J.D.'s little brother proved he could survive in the playground. And by the time J.D. left college, Hal was making a name for himself in sports at Douglass High. A knee injury dimmed Hal's promise as a football end, so he began to concentrate on basketball. In his senior year Hal led Douglass to the West Virginia state championship —the "Negro State Championship," that is. Douglass was an all-black high school, and sports in the state were divided into "white" and "Negro" at that time.

The year was 1954. Hal received scholarship offers from a dozen colleges. But the one that seemed most eager to have him was nearby Marshall University—a school that had never had anything but all-white teams. Marshall's basketball coach, Cam Henderson, wanted Hal to be the school's first black athlete. So did Hal's parents, friends, teachers and high school coach. Hal decided to give it a try.

It soon seemed clear that Greer had made the right move. At Marshall he became the first man to integrate a major college varsity team in West Virginia. Hal played with super-scorers like Charley Slack and Leo Byrd, and together they formed a solid group. Henderson drilled them thoroughly in zone defense. "We had a beautiful defense," remarked Greer. "All five starters thought as a unit. We each knew every move the others would make. And we played a run-and-shoot game."

Coach Henderson died during Greer's sophomore season. His death came as a shock to Hal, not only because he loved and respected the coach but because he wasn't sure how he would fit into the plans of Henderson's replacement, Jules Rivlin. But Greer didn't have to worry for long. Rivlin had no desire to upset the team's balance. In fact, he even increased Greer's role on the team.

"Hal was so humble—I think partially because of color—that he wouldn't shoot," Rivlin remembered. "He was averaging 55 percent and still he wouldn't shoot. I had to tell him if he didn't start to shoot he was going to sit on the bench."

After graduation Hal was picked up by the Syracuse Nationals of the NBA in the second round of the 1958 draft. The pro scene awed him. Although he had been a fine college guard, Greer had very little confidence. "I didn't think I had any chance at all," he said. "In fact, when I got to Syracuse, I didn't even unpack my bag."

Greer was particularly nervous because the administrators of the NBA had just banned zone defense, claiming it made for a slow game. The new rule, more than anything, made Greer uneasy. "I was a zone man—a zone man period. All of a sudden I had to play man-to-man, and I used to have horrible dreams about those big guys setting those picks in front of me."

So four years of college training had to be unlearned. Everything Rivlin had taught him about defense had to be set aside in a crash reeducation course. Instead of covering an area of the court as he had done in the Marshall zone, Greer learned to guard an individual player. Hal never forgot the lessons of his rookie year. "After a game," he said in 1965, "I think about the mistakes I made on defense that night. Sometimes I stay up all night thinking about defense, like after I've been chasing Oscar [Robertson] all over the court. That's enough to keep any man awake."

Hal Greer soars to the basket in his first season with the Syracuse Nationals.

As soon as he got the hang of playing man-to-man defense, Greer was anxious to prove himself. But Syracuse coach Paul Seymour had other ideas. "Paul would play me a quarter and then take me out and say, 'Now sit down and watch the veterans this quarter,' " Greer recalled.

One of the veterans Greer kept his eye on was the Nationals' superstar, Dolph Schayes. Hal sat on the bench watching Schayes much as he had once stood on the playground sidelines admiring his brother J.D. And once again Hal burned to get out there and play his own game. He wasn't jealous—just competitive. Schayes understood.

Looking back, Dolph explained: "Hal had this great talent, this exceptional gift of speed, and he couldn't understand why he was sitting on the bench. He just needed time to adjust to pro ball. But Hal said he had come to play not sit on the bench."

Hal didn't have to sit for long. By the end of the 1958–59 season he was a starter. And so began one of the truly brilliant careers in the NBA. A glance at his lifetime statistics clearly shows how brilliant it was. At the end of the 1971–72 season, Greer had played 14 years in the league. In that time, he had appeared in 1,084 games, passing all-time leader Dolph Schayes. He had attempted 18,596 field goals and made 8,413 of them. (Only Chamberlain and Baylor had attempted more, and only Chamberlain, Baylor and Robertson had made more.) Greer had played a total of 38,899 minutes, ranking behind Chamberlain and Bill Russell. He had 4,420 assists to his credit, placing him eighth in a group of super play-makers that included Robertson, Bob Cousy, Jerry West and Lenny Wilkens. He ranked second to Schayes in personal fouls, with 3,772. Neither man was a dirty player (as the category might suggest), just intense.

In 1963 the Syracuse Nationals moved south to Philadelphia and were renamed the 76ers. Featuring the aging Schayes and the young Greer, it was a good team and worthy of respect. But the 76ers got a surprisingly rude greeting from the fans in the town which called itself the "City of Brotherly Love." The crowds and the press seemed to avoid the team its first few years in town. The problem was that just a year earlier Philadelphia had "lost" its first NBA team, which was called the Warriors and starred Wilt Chamberlain. The Warriors had moved to San Francisco in hopes of attracting more spectators. The Philadelphia fans took out their frustration on the new 76ers.

Greer recalled: "The fans were used to the old Warriors. We [Syracuse] used to come here and beat them regularly. They were attached to Wilt. We suffered for something we were innocent of. I think it lasted two or three years."

At the end of the 1963–64 season Schayes re-

Hal Greer: basketball's most obscure 20,000-point man.

tired and the 76er management went shopping for a super attraction to take his place. And a super attraction was just what they got—Wilt Chamberlain! From a team standpoint it was an excellent deal. With Chamberlain, the Sixers had one of the two finest centers in the game.

And Wilt's faithful Philly fans were thrilled to get their hero back. But Hal Greer wasn't so happy. Once again he was reduced to second-banana status. This caused some rivalry between the two men —a rivalry that left little room for friendship. Still, Greer had to admit, "People come to see Wilt play. He's news. Whatever he says, whatever he does attracts the attention. What can you do?"

Hal did what he was used to doing—playing

great ball. He and Wilt teamed up to defeat the Warriors and the Boston Celtics in the 1967 championship playoffs, and the joy of playing on an NBA title team helped make up for the fact that Hal received little personal publicity.

In the 1968 All-Star game, Greer scored 19 points in the third quarter (an All-Star record) to rally the East squad to a 144–124 win, earning Most Valuable Player honors. It was Wilt who fed him for many of the buckets. After the game, Chamberlain told reporters: "Hal needs a certain amount of recognition to show people that he's on a par with Robertson and West. The MVP award will help prove he's one of the great guards in the game."

Greer was also one of the best shooters in the game. "Nobody in basketball," said one sportswriter, "is more deadly coming down the middle at full blast on the fast break, putting on the brakes at the foul line and going up for a jump shot. Next to a stuff shot by Wilt, it may be the surest two points in basketball."

Chamberlain was traded to the Lakers in 1968, and the two big men parted amiably. But by that time forward Billy Cunningham had established himself as Philadelphia's top hero. Greer and Cunningham got along up until the end of the 1971–72 season, when Billy left for the ABA.

Between 1958 and 1972, Greer averaged 19.5 points per game in the regular season and 20.4

No longer a starter in 1971, Greer comes off the 76er bench and drives past Boston's John Havlicek.

points in 92 playoff games. In addition, he appeared in ten consecutive All-Star contests from 1961 to 1970. His best year in a regular season was 1967–68, when he scored 1,976 points and averaged 24.1. But he really glittered in the 15 playoff games of 1967 that led to the championship, averaging 27.7 points in the title drive.

After the 1970–71 season, Hal made the switch from starter to sixth man behind younger, quicker men. Then he was named assistant coach to a succession of 76er coaches. Greer was the kind of man that the inexperienced players could look up to, and many people thought he would be a natural as a pro coach.

"I'm not looking for a job in the pros," Hal stated, "and I won't kick up any commotion to get one. But if the offer came along I would listen. I know the game. I also know how to handle men. That's the most important part of coaching the pros—handling men. Treat them as individuals, as adults. Treat them fair and honest. But be the boss."

Hal's retirement seemed close. But he knew that his body and his pride would let him know when it was really time to leave the game for good. "The back hurts, the legs hurt, the arms hurt. Even the fingers hurt. I won't stick around playing five minutes here, five minutes there. It's not my way. I couldn't do it," said the man who had done it all.

69

5.

Dave DeBusschere

Dave DeBusschere ran downcourt with the rest
of his New York teammates, turned, and prepared
to meet the offensive onrush of the Chicago Bulls.
The Chicago guard, wary of the famous Knick defense, slowly brought the ball upcourt. The other
four Bulls began their patterns. They weaved
among the Knicks, looking for an opening.

DeBusschere guarded his man, Chet Walker,
tightly. Walker ducked and dodged, ran and
stopped, in a futile attempt to shake free. The
Knick forward matched him step for step, move for
move, always keeping his body between Walker
and the ball.

Almost inevitably, the contest got more physical. The two men bumped one another hard. For a few seconds it was a stand-off, but then the duel appeared to be settled in Walker's favor—Dave took a mean shoulder from the Bull player and fell to the hard wood floor. Walker, left open at the foul line, took a pass. But before he could shoot, DeBusschere was back on his feet and crowding him.

Arms windmilling wildly, DeBusschere prevented his man from either passing off or dribbling around him. The 24-second clock was about to run out, and Walker finally had to shoot. He took the only shot available to him—a jumper. Anticipating his man's leap, Dave went up with him, arms stretched overhead. Walker arced his shot high to avoid DeBusschere's block, and the ball fell short of the target, bouncing off the front of the hoop.

Bob Love, the other Bull forward, grabbed the rebound beneath the basket and moved in for what looked like an easy lay-up. Out of nowhere, a Knick appeared, blocking Love's path. Unbelievably, it was Dave DeBusschere, who in a split second had abandoned Walker to confront Love. Love's desperation shot wasn't even close, and it was Dave DeBusschere who out-muscled the enemy center for the rebound.

Driving upcourt, Dave avoided the frantic efforts of the Bulls to slap the ball away. Spotting Knick center Willis Reed leading the fast break,

DeBusschere lobbed a long pass to him. Reed dunked for two New York points, and the 19,000 fans in Madison Square Garden went wild.

"Stop Dave from rebounding and scoring and you stop the Knicks," said Walker after the game. But the Bulls had been unable to stop DeBusschere, and they had lost.

Night after night, game after game, Dave was on the court giving his all for the Knicks—his stamina, his drive, his sweat. At 6-foot-6, and 225 pounds, he gave away inches in his battles under the boards. He wasn't sleek or fancy. He was no Spencer Haywood or Connie Hawkins—the kind of forwards who were always featured in the sports photos performing Globetrotter magic with the ball. Those were the one-on-one men with quick, snake-like moves that made them the idols of youngsters on concrete courts across the nation. The photos of DeBusschere were never very glamorous. Almost always the camera caught him straining to block out an opponent for the rebound or playing ferocious defense.

Defense was Dave's game, muscle was his tool. His job was to take on the other teams' highest-scoring forwards, and he frequently outplayed them. He became a perennial member of the

Caught by the camera in a typical pose, the New York Knicks' Dave DeBusschere strains for a rebound.

NBA's All-Defense Team, a tribute to his stalwart play and his power to intimidate foes. And he was a consistently good rebounder. Through the 1971–72 season, Dave had pulled down over 8,000 rebounds.

But defense certainly wasn't the only thing he had to offer. Dave's scoring average for his first ten years in the pros was a solid 15.6 points a game. Boston's Paul Silas, one of Dave's roughest opponents, once said: "DeBusschere's moves are not the greatest, but he has good moves if you play him too tight. What makes him tough on offense, though, is the way the Knicks move the ball so well. If you play him loose and take your eye off him, he'll sneak by you and get a pass in a fringe area for one of those five-foot jumpers. Or he'll get by you and be in position to tap in a rebound."

Dave's consistent scoring and super defense helped bring New York an NBA championship in 1970. That was DeBusschere's first pro championship, though he'd had plenty of experience playing for winners long before he entered the league.

In his boyhood days in Detroit, Dave was a superstar in two sports. At the age of 17, he was the top pitcher on a baseball team that captured a national junior championship. Two years later, his strong right arm took another amateur club to a national senior title. In between, he pitched Austin High School to a city Catholic championship and led the basketball team to a state crown. Those were days of action and excitement for Dave. He was the son of a tavern owner and grew up on a quiet street in east Detroit. But the days of real excitement lay ahead. Dave's talent in the two sports made him the target of college recruiters around the country. Out of loyalty and love for his native city, he chose the University of Detroit.

At the university Dave continued his winning ways in both sports. In his three years of varsity basketball he averaged 24.8 points a game. The squad flourished, attending one NCAA tournament and making it to the championship round of two National Invitational Tournaments. He also pitched the baseball team into three NCAA tournaments. DeBusschere's athletic contributions were so highly regarded that one of the school's lounges was named in his honor.

By the time he graduated in 1962, Dave was a sensation. General managers in two pro sports offered him contracts. "I was torn between baseball and basketball," recalled Dave. "I finally made a deal. I signed with the Detroit Pistons with the understanding I could play baseball, and I signed with the Chicago White Sox with the understanding I could play basketball."

The White Sox gave DeBusschere a $70,000 bonus for his services as a pitcher, and Detroit signed him for $15,000. He spent three years in the

White Sox organization. In 1963 he won three games and lost four for Chicago, and had a promising 3.11 ERA. But apparently that wasn't good enough for the Chicago management. Dave was sent down to the Sox' Triple-A club at Indianapolis for the 1964 and '65 seasons, where he continued to impress many of those around him. In those two years he posted a 25–9 record, and in 1965 he was second in strike-outs among all Triple-A pitchers.

On the basketball court DeBusschere fared somewhat better. He appeared in 80 games during his rookie year (1962–63), averaging twelve points a game for the Pistons. More important, he pulled down almost 700 rebounds and played standout defense for a first-year man. Piston owner Fred Zollner and general manager Don Wattrick were pleased with his play and the fine relationship he had with the team's veterans.

Thanks largely to DeBusschere, the Pistons reached the playoffs that year. Dave averaged 20 points a game in four postseason games. The following year was a disappointment because he was sidelined with a broken leg and could play in only 15 games. The Pistons fell to dead last in the NBA Western Division.

The Detroit management realized it had a dras-

Detroit rookie DeBusschere is one step ahead of the Hawks in this 1963 game.

tic problem—and came up with an equally drastic solution. In November 1964, the club announced that DeBusschere would replace Charley Wolf as Detroit's coach. Dave was 24 at the time, making him the youngest man ever to pilot a pro basketball team. "I was really surprised," he said, "but the team was down and I accepted."

A three-year contract worth $125,000 no doubt played a big part in Dave's decision to accept the job of player-coach. So did the apparent standstill of his baseball career. Angered at not being returned to Chicago after his successful 1964 season in the minors, Dave willingly left baseball after the summer of 1965.

Looking back years later, DeBusschere realized that he should never have tried to be a player-coach. Dave was younger than six of the ten men on his team, and as he explained: "I wasn't experienced enough to coach and handle men of this nature and caliber." He was the man in the middle: no longer just another player, yet too busy playing to learn his job as coach.

"It was a mistake, of course," said Ed Coil, who took over as general manager during De-Busschere's reign. "Dave was a good coach, but we were asking him to do too much: to be our high scorer among the big men, to be our best rebounder, to play the other side's highest-scoring forward—all this and be the coach."

The Pistons rose to next-to-last place in 1964–65, then dropped back into the basement the following year when a couple of key players were lost for the season. Throughout that frustrating time, DeBusschere did his best to keep his players' spirits up. He led by example. In a 1965 game against Philadelphia, for instance, Dave played 33 minutes, scored 15 points and snagged eight rebounds—with a 102-degree fever.

Though he appeared in 79 games in both 1964–65 and 1965–66 and averaged more than 16 points per game, Dave still wasn't satisfied with his development as a player. Neither was Ed Coil, who wanted Dave to play full time. So by mutual agreement, DeBusschere gave up coaching early in the 1966–67 season. The effect of the reduced pressure was immediate, and Dave had his finest scoring year as a pro, averaging 18.2 points. The next season he averaged 17.9 points and pulled down 1,081 rebounds, a personal high. Detroit even managed to make the playoffs in 1967–68.

Dave's star loomed very bright indeed in Detroit, so it was quite a shock to fans and newsmen alike when he was traded to New York in December 1968. He was sent to the Knicks for center Walt Bellamy and guard Howie Komives. "It's like being reborn," DeBusschere exclaimed when he heard of the deal. "I'll try to make New York a winner."

And that's exactly what he did. Willis Reed

switched from forward to center (replacing Bellamy) and quickly proved himself one of the league's best. Dave took Reed's forward spot, completing a unit that became famous for its solid team play. His style blended perfectly into coach Red Holzman's philosophy of unselfish hit-the-open-man play and defense, defense, defense!

It was no coincidence that the Knicks beat the Pistons just one day after Dave first put on a New York uniform. DeBusschere was the Knicks' top rebounder and scorer, and the fans in Detroit's Cobo Arena could have tarred and feathered Piston coach Paul Seymour for giving their hero away. And it was no coincidence that, with Dave's help, the Knicks reached the Eastern Division playoffs at the close of the season.

Although sportswriters often failed to give him full credit for his contributions, Dave DeBusschere became a cornerstone of the New York team almost from the moment he joined it in 1968. In his first four seasons with the Knicks (from 1968–69 through 1971–72) his points-per-game averages were 16.3, 14.6, 15.6 and 15.4. In that same period he averaged well over 800 rebounds a season.

Dave's unique value as the Knicks' "workhorse" was summed up by one observer who said, "DeBusschere is not the most important Knick. In fact, from a production standpoint, both Willis Reed and Walt Frazier rate ahead of him. But the

Dave DeBusschere: the complete basketball player.

importance of the stabilizing force which Dave exerts on New York should not be overlooked. Most fans miss it because it is done so quietly. But you can bet coach Red Holzman is grateful for it."

"Dave is the complete basketball player," agreed Holzman. "Sometimes he'll score only four or six points in 40 minutes. People say to me, 'How come you play him so long?' I say, 'Because he does a hell of a rebounding job for us.' If he can get the rebounds and play good defense, we've got other guys on this team who can shoot."

The 1969–70 season was, of course, the best of all for the rugged forward. The Knicks got off to a fast start in 1969 and were soon the scourge of the league. Along the way to their first NBA championship, the Knicks set a record for consecutive wins. Facing Cincinnati after 17 wins in a row, New York triumphed when Dave made a key interception in the final seconds. That was quite a game, but for New York fans nothing can compare to the drama of the fifth game of the playoff finals.

The Knicks were facing the Los Angeles Lakers in Madison Square Garden. Each team had won two playoff games. In the fifth game the Knicks were behind 25–15 with eight seconds left in the first quarter when disaster struck. Willis Reed, on whom New York depended heavily to neutralize the Lakers' massive Wilt Chamberlain, strained the muscles in his right hip going for a loose ball. Reed was taken out, and the Knicks' reserve centers, Nate Bowman and Bill Hosket, were no match for the 7-foot-2 Wilt. By half time New York was trailing badly. There seemed no possible way the Knicks could win.

But somehow they did. Incredibly, they beat the Lakers, 107–100. Insiders say that during half time Dave DeBusschere came up with the winning strategy. In the second half the Knicks used a double-post offense and double-teamed Chamberlain on defense, with DeBusschere and fellow forward Dave Stallworth doing the dirty work. Wilt was held scoreless for the whole second half.

New York (without Reed) lost the sixth playoff

DeBusschere uses some muscle to get by the Lakers' Happy Hairston, as big Wilt Chamberlain looks on.

game in Los Angeles, then returned home for the seventh and deciding match. Madison Square Garden was jam-packed with screaming Knick fans, and almost all eyes were on Willis Reed. Though the New York captain had not fully recovered from his painful injury, he wasn't about to miss the crucial finale. The sight of their big center courageously dragging himself up and down the court inspired team and fans alike. And Reed's presence in the middle—confronting Chamberlain—allowed DeBusschere to work in the corners.

And work he did! His outside shooting kept the Lakers off balance. His solid defense nullified LA's star forward, Elgin Baylor. Willis couldn't go to the boards effectively, so Dave took up the burden of the rebounding.

When the game ended the Knicks had their first NBA title, 113–99. Though Reed's valiant return captured most of the headlines, no one could ignore DeBusschere's contributions. He had scored 18 points and pulled down a team-leading 17 rebounds in another superb performance.

Those steady performances continued for years, keeping New York a winner and enhancing Dave's reputation among his fellow pros. Said Los Angeles' Bill Bridges: "There's not one other guy in this league who gives the 100 percent DeBusschere does—every night, every game, at both ends of the court."

6.

Roger Brown

Many basketball fans are familiar with the Connie Hawkins story. Connie was the most celebrated schoolyard player ever to come out of New York. In his first year at the University of Iowa, he was called for questioning in a gambling scandal. Although he was not accused of any wrong-doing, he was pressured into leaving college and banned from playing ball in the NBA. Connie played in the short-lived American Basketball League and later in the ABA. But he also sued the NBA, arguing that it had no right to keep him from playing. The league finally settled, and Connie found wealth and stardom with the Phoenix Suns.

Few people realize that Roger Brown was

banned from the NBA at the same time as Hawkins. Perhaps because Brown stayed in the ABA, his story didn't receive as much attention as Connie's did. Yet Roger went through the same agonies as his Brooklyn buddy. For several years, in fact, it appeared that Brown would never get to play pro ball anywhere.

Roger was a freshman at the University of Dayton when his world caved in. The time was May 1961. He (along with Connie Hawkins and others) was called for questioning in a gambling investigation by the District Attorney of New York. Both players had been high school stars in nearby Brooklyn. The investigators suggested that they cooperated with gamblers, introducing them to college players who might shave points (win games by fewer points), so that the gamblers could win big bets. The men accused of paying off the players were Joseph Hacken, a gambler, and Jack Molinas, a former pro basketball player. Hawkins had introduced Brown to the two men in 1959.

"I was accused of taking $250 for 'good services,'" Brown told a reporter. "The $250 is a lie, and my testimony is on record in the New York grand jury. It was 70 bucks for food and gas. They bought me a meal now and then and gave me gas money, and sometimes I'd take a friend along to eat.

"Hacken acted like everybody else who

watched the playground pickup games. He'd see some kid he didn't know and ask if I'd introduce him. So I did. When I was ready to go to college, he came to me and asked a certain question. I'd rather not say what it was, but I think you can figure it out. I only saw him once after that. It was in a restaurant and not by arrangement."

Hacken and Molinas were sent to jail. Brown and Hawkins were never accused or tried for any wrong-doing. The District Attorney later said he was satisfied that neither of them had done anything wrong.

Yet the gambling investigation changed Brown's life. Like Hawkins, he was pressured into leaving college. He was outlawed from NCAA games, which meant he couldn't play for *any* college team. And he was banned for life from the National Basketball Association, the only big-time pro league in existence at that time. Roger's days as a basketball player seemed to be over.

Roger had come from the slums of Brooklyn's Brownsville section, where basketball had been a way of life for him since elementary school. "We'd go to different playgrounds every day," he recalled. "You'd play basketball 26 hours a day—you couldn't get away from it."

The game was more than a sport—it was one of the few ways a boy could move up and out of the rough-and-tumble life of the ghetto. The other big

Roger Brown: the "prince" of city basketball.

game in the neighborhood was craps, in which a shrewd gambler could win big money. Roger had tried his hand at the dice game, but he said, "Craps never really paid off. Sometimes, when you won, you got your butt whipped. There was always a guy around the corner when you wanted to go home. You had to pay to get by. Might as well give him the money than get beat up. You had to be a track star to get out of there. I got chased quite a bit, but I was a good runner. I stuck with basketball because it was a lot more fun."

Brown became a great player in high school and on the playgrounds. If Connie Hawkins was the "king" of the city courts, then Roger was the "prince." Starring for Brooklyn's Wingate High, Roger set the New York City record for career points, a record that stood for years. Wingate's big rival for the city's public school championship was Boys High. Its star was Connie Hawkins.

The two schools and the two schoolboy stars met in the finals of the 1959 city championship tournament. The place was Madison Square Garden. Although Hawkins and Brown had met many times in playground games, this was one of the few times they played face to face in an official game.

Hawkins had outplayed Brown many times in the playgrounds, but that night it was a different story. Connie guarded Brown tightly but only succeeded in picking up fouls. Time and time again, Roger would drive Hawkins into a Wingate pick (block), then shoot in his split-second of freedom. The whole Wingate strategy was to get the ball to Brown. Hawkins began to tighten up. His offense was off. By the end of the third quarter, he had fouled out of the game. Boys High finished the game on top, 62–59, but Brown won the war of the giants. He had scored 38 points to Hawkins' 18.

Brown enjoyed playing in Madison Square Garden. In fact, that was one reason he chose the University of Dayton out of the pile of college scholarship offers he received. Dayton was always one of the basketball teams participating in the National Invitational Tournament held at the Garden every year. Roger had visions of returning home and playing to a crowd of friends and relatives. He liked to think that one day, when he was through with college, he would play in the Garden on a regular basis, starring for the New York Knicks.

But then, before he had even caught on with the freshman team at the University of Dayton, Brown's dreams of glory came to a shattering end. After the gambling investigation, he was forced out of college. The university seemed more interested in protecting its own reputation than in doing justice to Roger Brown.

Since Roger wouldn't be allowed to play college basketball (his only hope for a scholarship), he didn't bother applying to other schools. Instead, he settled in the city of Dayton and went to work in a General Motors plant. Those were hard days for Brown. He made decent money, but all the cash in the universe couldn't make up for his lost dreams and ambitions.

Roger played amateur basketball a couple of times a week. It was a way to keep in shape and, more important, to keep in touch with the game he loved. Sometimes he journeyed to Cincinnati to watch the Royals play. Those were bittersweet trips. On one hand, he enjoyed watching the best players in the game. But it was hard to accept the fact that he would never be down on the court with them.

If he had wanted to, Brown could have played at least one season of pro ball. In 1961 the American Basketball League was formed by Abe Saperstein, founder of the Harlem Globetrotters. Connie Hawkins played with the ABL's Pittsburgh franchise. The New York franchise, the Tuck Tapers, wanted Roger to play for them. But the ABL was a poor league. "They offered me $5,500," Brown recalled. "I could make more money operating a machine at General Motors."

Roger rejected the ABL, and the league folded midway through its second season. Brown continued to work at his G.M. job for six years.

The college scandal had left Roger secretive and distrustful. Over the years his bitterness faded somewhat, but he never really forgot that unhappy time. "I'll always hold something back and I'll always have a shell," he admitted. "If you look for the worst, you won't get hurt."

Roger certainly expected the worst when the ABA was organized in 1967. He had seen how the ABL's early failure had shaken Connie Hawkins, and Brown wasn't about to let himself in for another disappointment.

Mike Storen, who was then the vice-president and general manager of the ABA's Indiana Pacers, sought out Roger. The new league, unlike the NBA, was willing to give Brown a chance. The Pacers offered a lot more money than the Tuck Tapers, but Roger still hesitated. Oscar Robertson, a native of Indianapolis (the Pacers' home), helped persuade him to join the club. Brown became the first player to sign with the team and one of the first to sign with the ABA.

Even then, Roger wasn't sure he had made the right decision. In fact, the day he signed his contract with the Pacers, he went to work on the night shift at the factory. Instead of quitting his job he took a leave of absence to go to Indiana's training camp. "I tried to protect myself all the way around," he explained, "so if I didn't make it at camp I had a job to go back to. I had five years of seniority, and I didn't want to throw that away for a chance that might fold in a week and leave me right back where I started."

Brown had no trouble making the team. He was a starter almost from the very moment he set foot in camp. And the ABA didn't fold in a week. So General Motors lost a good worker, and pro basketball gained a great player.

Just how great was best illustrated in the 1969–70 season—Roger's finest year ever. He played in all 84 regular-season games, led the Pacers in scoring with a 23.1-point average and made 81 percent of his free throws. Indiana breezed into the playoffs

Brown (#35) gets all tangled up in the final round of the 1970 ABA playoffs.

with a 59–25 record. And then Roger really broke loose.

The Pacers' opponents in the finals were the Los Angeles Stars (they later moved to Utah). The Stars were surprisingly strong in the six matches, but they didn't have a chance against red-hot Roger Brown. The Brooklyn bomber almost tore them apart single-handedly. "He was just super," raved Bill Sharman, who was then coaching the Stars. "The last three games: 53, 39, 45. And it seemed like he'd come down and make that big play every time."

The numbers Sharman mentioned were the points Roger scored in the fourth, fifth and sixth games. The 53-point total set an ABA record at the time.

The fifth game of the series was on national television, and people who had never seen an ABA game were treated to an astounding display of offensive fireworks by the 6-foot-4 forward. The Stars double- and sometimes triple-teamed Brown, but that didn't stop him. An excellent passer, Roger simply threw the ball to an open man whenever the Stars ganged up on him. When LA jammed the lanes, he just pulled up short and popped in one of his 15-foot jump shots.

Roger's ball-handling skill made the Stars dizzy. As often as possible, the Pacers would isolate Brown offensively, allowing him to go one-on-one with his man. On one play the Pacer guards brought the ball down the court slowly. Then four of the Pacers broke to the right side of the court, taking their men with them. Brown was alone on the left side, guarded by a single Star. He caught a quick pass and went to work.

You had to be watching very closely to catch it all. Roger didn't move a single step. Instead, he threw cobra-fast head fakes. First, he snapped his head to the right, to the inside. The forward guarding him leaned inside. Brown then gave another quick head fake, this time to the outside. That was all it took. His opponent was so nervous he jumped to the outside, leaving the inside wide open. Roger drove to the basket for an unmolested lay-up.

In the 15 postseason games, he averaged 28.5 points a game. Thanks largely to Brown, Indiana won its first ABA championship.

"Roger Brown," Sharman told reporters after the series, "is the closest thing to Elgin Baylor, when Elgin was at his peak—the way he handles the ball and shoots, his great ability changing direction and speed. One-on-one, he's as good as there is. And he makes all those tough plays look easy. A lot of players can come down on the fast break and make an easy play look spectacular. You know, like a Maravich, or even a Cousy. It's fun to watch and you 'oooh' and 'aaah.' But Roger, like Oscar Robertson, will come down and make a real tough play and do it so nonchalantly that you'll think it was an easy one."

Brown's hallmark was consistency on offense. In his first five seasons with the Pacers, the team made the playoffs every year. Roger averaged 19.6, 21, 23.1, 20.6 and 18.5 points in regular-season play. And every year his playoff averages were even better: 21.7, 27, 28.5, 21.8, and 20.4 points per game. When the pressure was on, Roger was at his best.

The pressure was definitely on during the middle of the 1971–72 season. Indiana's starting guards were both under 6-foot-1, and they were having trouble handling the league's taller backcourt men. The Pacers' solution was to move Roger into one of the guard spots. At 6-foot-4, he was a little short for a forward but he was a big guard. Brown played the position up until the playoffs, when he moved back to his familiar corner post and helped Indiana win another title.

Brown had little trouble at the guard position, but the forward spot was where he really shone. And it was as a forward that he led the Pacers in assists his first four years on the team.

"I'd have to say I've gotten a lot smarter in the game and a lot more confident," Brown explained. "That first year I drove to the basket 80 percent of the time. But I found my shots getting blocked. Now I pull up and shoot the jumper. Out of the forward slot, I think the most important thing in the pro game today is knowing when to shoot. Now when I go out there I feel there's no one I can't score on, that's the kind of confidence I've got."

That kind of confidence was a long time coming. It had taken many years after the collapse of his college career for Roger Brown to find his place

Brown goes up for a shot as the Pacers defeat the New York Nets in the 1972 playoffs.

in the pros. He never did become a Knick, and Madison Square Garden was never his home court. Was he disappointed?

The answer to that question may be found in the law suit he leveled at the NBA. In 1966, Connie Hawkins brought suit against the older league for blacklisting him. The Hawk's suit was for 6.5 million dollars, and he stood an excellent chance of collecting every penny of it. Almost three years after the suit was filed, though, Hawkins and the NBA came to a deal. The league not only agreed to let him play, but handed him a 1.5 million dollar contract in the bargain.

Brown's suit was for 1.5 million. But, unlike his pal, Roger wanted no part of the NBA. "The Pacers and the ABA gave me the opportunity to play professional basketball," he explained. "I started here and certainly expect to play for the Pacers until I retire. Indianapolis is a great town, and our goal is to once again bring the title home."

On another occasion Brown added, "I want to clear my name. I have no intention of jumping."

Roger loved Indianapolis, and Indianapolis loved him. The city proved its love twice in one day—Election Day, 1971. The Pacers were playing the Carolina Cougars that afternoon. Brown had an outstanding game—24 points and 19 rebounds. He even scored eight straight in the last moments to ice the Indiana victory, 137–116. The home fans cheered him as loud as they always did.

But that wasn't Brown's only victory. After the game, he learned that the townspeople had also cheered him at the polls. He had run for a seat in the Indianapolis City Council and won that, too.

Roger explained his commitment to civic affairs: "Politics and law enforcement are everybody's responsibility. Basketball players are no exception. I am concerned about the crime and poverty and political apathy plaguing our community. I was fortunate to escape those evils in Brooklyn, and I am determined to do my best to erase them here. As a successful basketball star I can be a more objective politician because I'm economically secure. My main professional job is basketball, but my political responsibility is to the people I represent."

Besides being on the city council, Brown was a deputy coroner in Indianapolis and a member of a citizens group that acted as a link between the police and the people. One of Roger's voluntary duties was to ride along with police as they made their rounds. "I think it helps when a person with my kind of name rides in a police car. People recognize me and are apt to be calmer."

With all his civic activities, it was amazing that Brown had had any time left to play ball. But he found the time—and the energy and the incentive. A boost to that incentive was provided by what Roger called "the best multi-year contract in pro basketball." Other players might have been paid more in outright salaries, but Brown got a good part of his income from a clause that made him a part-owner of the Pacer organization. It was no drop in the bucket, either. The Pacers were one of the top five money-making franchises in all of pro basketball.

It had been a steep climb for Brown—from the depths of disappointment and bitterness to the heights of pro basketball stardom. As the Pacers and the ABA prospered, it seemed only fitting that Brown should share the credit and the glory with the team and the league that gave him a chance to prove his basketball mastery. Despite the years of adversity and injustice, Roger Brown had finally come out on top.

7.

Lenny Wilkens

No man alive could speak about the roles of the guard and the coach in pro basketball as clearly as Lenny Wilkens. "A guard," he explained, "is a guy who has to run the show out there, like a quarterback in football. He's the guy that controls the tempo of the game by running the offense, the guy who gets the fast break going or slows the team down when things aren't going too well."

Wilkens, one of the NBA's all-time assist leaders, said of his work: "If another guard is pressuring me in the backcourt, I can get the ball up all right. But the important thing is to have something in mind when I get over the ten-second line.

"The key to play-making is penetration. You

have to make things happen. You don't just complete plays that are there. You create situations through your movement. I try to bring the ball—to penetrate—at least to the foul line. From there I have the ability to make my shot consistently against my man, and he has to have help. When he gets that help, somebody's free. It's my job to get him the ball."

Lenny knew about coaching from experience, too. From 1969 through 1971–72 he was the player-coach of the Seattle SuperSonics. According to Wilkens: "There is nothing like respect on a basketball team—toward the coach, toward one another. And I tried to set an example. The big thing Bill Russell did as coach of the Celtics was to be an example, to give 100 percent every night. My fellows know that I'll give up the ball, that I'll pass. That makes it easier for them to do the same. From a coaching standpoint, there are certain things you want done, so you relate them to your guard. Since I've also been in that position, I know what I want done."

Wilkens first got involved with basketball in the early 1950s, when he joined the Holy Rosary Church team in a Catholic Youth Organization (CYO) league in Brooklyn. Holy Rosary was one of the best teams in the circuit, rolling from one championship to another. And Lenny was responsible for much of the squad's success. Nicknamed

Lenny Wilkens: a true "team" player.

"Lefty" by his buddies, Wilkens practiced his skills in cramped basement gyms and on concrete courts. Because of his small size he couldn't dominate the bigger fellows, but he did learn how to control the flow of the game from his backcourt position. Wilkens learned the importance of team play early.

Lenny's best friend in the old days was a boy who went on to become a major league baseball star—Tommy Davis. The two athletes remained friends long after they left the neighborhood and entered the pros. "Lenny and I grew up together in Bedford-Stuyvesant," Davis said. "I remember when he started playing basketball. He played in a

103

league with fellows who outweighed him by 40 and 50 pounds. I'm not too much of an idol worshipper; but seeing him play as a kid, I became a wholehearted worshipper and fan of Lenny Wilkens."

Mention the name Bedford-Stuyvesant to any New Yorker and he'll immediately picture a black ghetto in Brooklyn—a place of urban decay, tough street gangs and violence. It's terribly difficult for a youngster to emerge from such an environment unharmed. But Lenny Wilkens did it. He shrugged off his neighborhood's terrible reputation. "Bedford-Stuyvesant wasn't as bad as people make it out to be," Lenny explained. "Maybe it was to people who didn't live there. But it wasn't a ghetto to me. It was where I lived. You adjust."

One man who lived there and saw plenty of young people like Lenny destroyed by the bad schools and the temptation to commit crimes and use drugs, was Father Thomas Mannion. He was the coach of the Holy Rosary Church team and a lifelong friend of Lenny's. "It's a mystery to me how a kid makes it under those circumstances," said Father Mannion. "But of all the people I've met, Lenny is the most unique. I've seen kids with more ability who couldn't offset the poverty. Almost from the beginning—I have this mental picture of him as a little guy—he was able to attract kids, to lead. He had an impact on the entire neighborhood. The kids respected him deeply. He had the rare ability to get all the boys to recognize the benefit to the team and to themselves if they played as a team. He knew how to make things work."

Both Lenny and Tommy Davis attended Boys High in Brooklyn. Davis was outstanding on the basketball court and urged his friend to join him there. But because he had to work after school when the practice sessions were held, Len didn't go out for the team until his junior year.

Lenny's entrance into high school ball was just short of a disaster. The Boys High basketball coach was Mickey Fisher, a strong-willed, strict disciplinarian. He demanded absolute obedience from his players and received it by hounding them unmercifully. Fisher was a man who put all his energy into coaching, and he got results. Other pro basketball stars like Connie Hawkins and Sihugo Green also played under Fisher at Boys High.

The transition from church team to high school team was a difficult one for Wilkens. He couldn't adjust to Fisher's way of doing things, and he was frequently the victim of the coach's outbursts. Lenny took it hard. He was a sensitive boy, not used to loud criticism. So one day he quit the team to go back to his after-school job—and to get away from Fisher.

It wasn't until the middle of the next basketball season (his senior year) that he finally gave in to the urging of his best friend. "Come on out and play," Tommy prompted. "You know Mickey didn't mean it. You can make this team. We need you."

So Lenny returned. "All I wanted to do was play basketball," he explained. "I saw guys from college playing in the parks, and I wanted to go places and see places and do the things they did. That was my incentive."

Lenny finally learned how to get along with Mickey Fisher, and in his last half-season at Boys High he averaged eleven points a game and became the real quarterback of the team. "He was great," recalled Davis. "You didn't know he was around, but he stole the ball and made the shots. I was just a garbageman."

For college Lenny chose Providence, or rather it chose him. By the time he graduated from high school in 1956, the local colleges knew of Wilkins' fine reputation as a player. But those outside the New York area had never even heard his name. Father Mannion changed that by writing to coach Joe Mullaney of Providence, a Catholic college in Rhode Island. Mannion thought Lenny should get away from the city. And Providence, with its fine academic and athletic program, seemed an ideal place. Mullaney scouted Wilkens in a CYO tournament and offered him a full scholarship.

Being one of the few black students on campus

took a bit of getting used to, but Lenny adjusted. In fact, he was soon one of the most popular boys around. And he did all right on the academic front, too. An average student in high school, Lenny worked hard and made Dean's List in college. Most important, he gained a national reputation for his play-making and defense on the basketball team.

"He played the left wing on our combination defense," remembered coach Mullaney, who later became boss of the ABA's Kentucky Colonels. "We set it up like a 1–3–1 zone and then it became man-to-man. It got so the other teams never brought the ball up on Lenny's side."

In one game, against St. Joseph's, Providence was down by five points in the last minute of play. Lenny stole the ball three times and fed teammates for baskets and a winning margin of one point. "St. Joe's couldn't believe it," said Mullaney. "He had stolen the game away."

Wilkens graduated in 1960 and was the number one draft pick of the NBA's St. Louis Hawks. Everyone wished him luck, but many, including Mullaney, felt he would have a tough time making it in pro ball. Just 6-foot-1 and 185 pounds, Lenny seemed even smaller in the land of the giants, and he had never been much of a shooter.

But Lenny surprised almost everyone by sticking with St. Louis for eight years. The Hawks

LENNY WILKENS

were perennial Western Division leaders (they had won three consecutive division titles prior to 1960) with a formidable front wall and a weak backcourt. At forward they had All-Star performers in Bob Pettit and Cliff Hagan. Brawny Clyde Lovellette was their center. St. Louis needed a take-charge guard to pull the team together—and, naturally, to get the ball to the big men. Lenny was that man.

Lenny didn't really look the part. With his smiling, boyish face, he didn't inspire instant respect from the veterans. He made plenty of mistakes, as rookies do. However, it was the fact that he never got mad at himself for committing an error that made St. Louis coach Paul Seymour angry. Seymour took Lenny's calm, businesslike manner as a sign that the youngster didn't care.

The turning point in Wilkens' career with the Hawks came early in January 1961. Until that time Len had only been a spot starter, and he was fed up with riding the bench. He was making some spectacular shots one practice session when Seymour came over and asked why he didn't shoot that way in the real games.

"How would you know?" the rookie bristled. "I don't play long enough for you to find out. I make a mistake and out I come."

Playing for St. Louis, Wilkens gets fouled by a Chicago player on a lay-up attempt.

Seymour said nothing but seemed happy that the rookie had finally shown some fire. In the next game Lenny played the full 48 minutes—mistakes and all. And from then on he was a starter.

In 1960–61 the Hawks won their last division title, but after that St. Louis was never again the same team. Coaches came and went. Players retired and were cut and traded. Only one thing remained constant—Lenny Wilkens' superb play.

From his third season on, Lenny was always one of the top ten in NBA assists. In his eight years with the Hawks he averaged 15.9 points a game and had a total of 3,048 assists. He was named team captain in 1965 and finally started to get some recognition. Men in the know began favorably comparing him to the league's other top guards.

"You mention Robertson, West and Greer and you've got to mention Lenny in the same breath," said Richie Guerin, the Hawks' coach. "O's a little bit better—and possibly West—but Lenny doesn't take much of a back seat to them."

"What is a superstar?" asked St. Louis center Zelmo Beaty, Lenny's roommate. "A superstar does everything, right? Well, Lenny's our superstar —like Oscar. Lenny's our leader. He's good for morale. If you're going bad, he asks you: 'What can I do?' He gets you loose for the lay-up, just to get you generated, to get you to the hoop. He juggles the four of us and takes care of himself, too."

But Lenny wanted more than praise. "If people

are saying that I'm not far behind Robertson and those other backcourt men and superstars, I want to be close to them in salary," he complained.

Lenny was a discontented man in 1967–68. He'd had a bitter—and public—contract quarrel with Hawks owner Ben Kerner. Despite his unhappiness, it turned out to be Wilkens' finest season with St. Louis. He wound up second in the league in assists (8.2 a game) and averaged 20 points per game. But by the start of the next season Lenny and the Hawks had parted company. The Hawks went south, to Atlanta and bigger crowds. Lenny was traded to the expansion Seattle SuperSonics for forward Walt Hazzard.

Wilkens' first year with the Sonics was simply super. He was second in NBA assists for the second consecutive year, and ninth in scoring, with 22.4 points per game. But the team won only 30 games, and coach Al Bianchi resigned.

Seattle needed a coach—someone who was a leader and knew the game. Lenny was a natural choice. On August 6, 1969, Dick Vertlieb, then the Sonics' general manager, made the announcement.

Wilkens was only the NBA's second black coach (Bill Russell was the first). "Lenny's race never entered my mind," said Vertlieb, "and personally I don't think it's relevant at all. He's had a superstar rating, and everyone respects him."

Len asked for, and received, a one-year contract as coach, so he could return to his multi-year player contract if things didn't work out. But, of course, they did work out. True, in 1969–70 the club won just 36 games under his rule. But for the first time, Seattle fielded a cohesive unit, a competitor.

Wilkens made Seattle a winner. It took time, but he accomplished it by instituting a program of tough physical and mental conditioning. By constantly urging his teammates to play unselfish ball and leading by example. By taking stern measures when needed.

One night in 1970, for example, he fined every member of the Sonics—including himself—$100 following a 129–128 loss to the Detroit Pistons. "Some of the guys," he explained, "had broken elementary rules of training. I fined the innocent with the guilty. Basketball is so much a team game, I wanted the innocent ones to ride the guilty."

There were good nights too, of course. In one game, the SuperSonics whipped Lenny's old team, the Atlanta Hawks, 130–107. It was a memorable evening because the slim player-coach, driving ferociously to his left as only he could do, bombed home 41 points (a career high). All the while, his right leg was heavily bandaged to ease a painfully pulled hamstring muscle. The other players did their best to help, running the bigger and more physical Hawks ragged.

"What I like about being a player-coach,"

A SuperSonic super-guard, Lenny drives for the basket against the Cleveland Cavaliers.

Lenny told reporters, "is that everybody on the team becomes involved because you need help. They're all looking to help you, and they help themselves that way."

The season's statistics show that Lenny did plenty of helping, too. His scoring dropped to 17.8 points per game while his assists rose to 9.1, tops in the league. Rather than hog the ball, he passed off to his teammates and showed them how to hit the open man.

Lenny enjoyed tremendous popularity among his players. Former Sonic Tom Meschery explained, "When Lenny became player-coach, we became a better team. Suddenly, he was responsible for everyone on the team, not just himself, and his scoring went down. But it didn't matter to Lenny. He's completely unselfish as a player and as a coach, and the only thing that bothered him was losing. When things were going bad, he blamed himself. When things were going well, he gave all the credit to the other players."

Seattle won 38 games in 1970–71 and continued to improve. Lenny himself was still making plays at a phenomenal rate of 9.2 a game. He was named to the West squad in the 1971 NBA All-Star game. There he scored 21 points (the game high) and took control of the West squad with what one reporter called "an incredible display of dribbling wizardry and shooting genius that brings to life the realiza-

Wilkens jumps high to score two of his 21 points in the 1971 All-Star game. At left, another star of the West, Bob Love of Chicago.

tion of what a great player Wilkens has been." At the end of the game, Lenny was named Most Valuable Player.

In 1971–72 the Sonics just missed the playoffs. But under Lenny's guidance, they wound up with the finest record of their short history—47 wins and 35 losses. Wilkens finished with 9.6 assists per game, second highest in the NBA that year.

Lenny was ready to step down as a coach before the end of the 1971–72 campaign. He had sometimes described the burden of being a player-coach as "heavy" and "disturbing." He and the Seattle owners agreed that since the team had developed a winning attitude, they could bring in a new coach and let Lenny return to being just a player.

But the management took things a step further. They decided to go completely with youth in the backcourt. Lenny was traded to the Cleveland Cavaliers for a young guard, Butch Beard. Wilkens was very unhappy with the trade. He loved Seattle—the team, the fans, the town. He sat out the first few weeks of the 1972–73 season before joining the Cavs.

But Cleveland, a youthful expansion team like Seattle, needed Lenny to pull things together. And it was the challenge that finally put him in a Cavalier uniform. For Lenny Wilkens was a man who never, never turned his back on a challenge.

8.

Charlie Scott

"I can remember the first basketball game I ever watched on TV. It was the Knicks against Philadelphia when Philadelphia had Wilt [Chamberlain]. I remember that Kenny Sears made a shot from the corner and the Knicks won. Everybody got so excited, but I couldn't figure out why. It didn't mean anything to me. I was trying to get everyone outside to play stickball."

Charlie Scott never did have much luck getting his friends to play stickball. Maybe it was because he grew up in Harlem, a place where basketball has always been king. Eventually he got tired of urging his buddies to come run the bases (the manhole covers, that is). They were too busy tossing the big, brown ball through the hoop to think about other games. So, since Charlie couldn't beat 'em, he joined 'em. And the result was marvelous.

Scott could have been a good baseball player. When he was in high school, the major leagues scouted him. Instead, he became a great basketball player—perhaps the finest young guard in the pro game. He proved it first in two seasons with the Virginia Squires of the ABA and then with the NBA's Phoenix Suns.

Reminiscing about the days in his old neighborhood, Charlie said, "Once you start playing basketball, it brings out all the competitiveness in you. I mean, it's you against someone else. Each individual can do so much on his own."

That was the basis of schoolyard basketball in New York City. You against someone else. One-on-one. Self reliance. That's the way Scott approached the game, and it's the way he approached his life. He was criticized for his outspoken behavior as often as he was praised for his outstanding play. But neither praise nor blame changed him one bit. Growing up in the slums he learned that you had to face things squarely or get stepped on. He carried that bitter lesson throughout his life.

Charlie was brought up in a rough section of a rough ghetto. "You couldn't go out of that area unless you were looking for a fight," he recalls.

A boy growing up there had few choices. He

Charlie Scott: one-on-one on the court and off.

could hide in his apartment; he could join a gang, which Charlie did for a while; or he could retreat into a fantasy world through drugs. Although Charlie managed to stay away from the drug world, many of his acquaintances weren't as lucky. One boy who was admired throughout the neighborhood for his moves on the basketball court dropped out that way. "The last time I saw him," Scott said grimly, "he was all swollen up with dope." But, of course, there was still one other choice—basketball.

119

CHARLIE SCOTT

Charlie chose early. At Frederick Davidson Junior High, he averaged a whopping 52 points a game. Naturally, he expected to jump straight into varsity ball when he got to high school. But there he was disappointed. When he began his freshman year at Stuyvesant High, Charlie asked the varsity coach where he could sign up. The coach told him that freshmen played on the freshman team.

Charlie was indignant. He felt that freshman ball was beneath him. Besides, the varsity had won only one game the year before. "I decided that if I wasn't allowed to play varsity ball, then I wouldn't play any ball. I decided to transfer," he said.

Transfer he did. A friend of his, Jimmy Walker, had spent his high school days at Laurinburg Prep in North Carolina and then become an All-America at Providence College. Walker persuaded Charlie to go south to Laurinburg.

If Charlie had any hopes of becoming an instant star at Laurinburg, he was disappointed once again. The team was loaded with talent. The other boys were so good that one all-city player from New York never saw any action. Scott managed to get a few minutes playing time each game as a center, but he really wasn't suited for that position. He was a skinny 6-foot-3, and though his scoring was fine (16 points per game), he was a very weak rebounder.

Things improved the following year. He was

switched to guard—a spot where he could use his one-on-one magic—and became a starter. Laurinburg lost only one game that year, and Scott's scoring average went up to 22 points.

Laurinburg was undefeated during Scott's senior year. He contributed 27 points a game to an offense that averaged 110. But basketball wasn't Charlie's whole life. He worked as hard in the classroom as he did on the court. Laurinburg was a good school, and it brought out his ambitions. Scott knew he wanted to play ball for a career, but he also wanted to do more. He began thinking about becoming a doctor or a lawyer.

Long before Charlie graduated from Laurinburg, he was on the "must get" lists of several college scouts. Schools all around the country were eager to have him. Scott, however, was toying with the idea of staying in the South—or going to a college that had never had a black man on its basketball team. Some big white Southern schools also thought the time had come to integrate their teams and that Charlie might be the man to do it.

Scott visited several campuses, but once he saw the University of North Carolina at Chapel Hill, his search was over. "I fell in love with the place and the people," he said. He became one of a hundred black students in a student body of 15,000.

"Sure I was apprehensive," he said. "It was such a great challenge. You know people are going to be looking at you to see what you can do. You know they judge others by you. It had to be done by somebody."

Charlie was well liked by the Tar Heel fans, and his playing left little doubt that North Carolina had made a wise choice. But things weren't always easy for Scott. When North Carolina visited the campus of its arch-rival South Carolina, some fans shouted at him: "To hell with you, nigger! Go back to Harlem with your black buddies!" Scott also received some hate mail and even a few death threats.

But Charlie kept his cool and concentrated on his studies. He maintained a B-plus average and was on the Dean's List the whole time he was there. And, of course, there was his game. Playing in the shadow of senior All-America Larry Miller, sophomore Scott carved out a 17.6 point-per-game average and won all-conference honors. Then it was on to the 1968 Summer Olympics.

Many black athletes considered boycotting the Games. One of their complaints was that South Africa (which allowed no blacks on its teams) be banned from the competition. Although South Africa was finally eliminated, a number of blacks still chose to stay away. But Charlie decided to attend the trials. "You always want to know how you compare to the big-name players—guys like Rick Mount, Pete Maravich and Calvin Murphy," he said. "At the time I was just another player who was lucky to be invited. Then the team was chosen, and it became another challenge to prove that all those people who were picking us to lose were wrong." And they certainly were wrong. Charlie helped the team to a gold medal.

After his Olympic triumph no one was foolish enough to predict that Scott would have a bad junior year. He gave the Tar Heels 22.3 points a game and enough hustle to fill a dozen backcourts. But Charlie really turned it on in postseason play. In the Atlantic Coast Conference (ACC) Tourney, North Carolina beat Duke, 85–74, for their third consecutive championship. Scott scored 40 points in the game (28 in the second half) to guide the Tar Heels back from an eleven-point deficit. Then in the NCAA's Eastern Regional Tournament he contributed 22 points in a victory over Duquesne—and 32 points, including a game-winning jump shot, in a triumph over Davidson—for the Tar Heels' third straight crown in that series.

By all accounts it was an unbelievable year, one that Scott should have been able to savor for a long time. But Scott wasn't happy. When the conference newspapermen made their annual choice of ACC Player of the Year, they picked sophomore John Roche of South Carolina. Roche, who later joined the ABA's New York Nets, was also the only unanimous all-conference selection. And, to top things off, South Carolina's Frank McGuire—not North

At the University of North Carolina, Scott led the Tar Heels to a string of Atlantic Coast Conference titles.

Carolina's Dean Smith—was chosen ACC Coach of the Year.

When Charlie heard about the selections, he exploded—calling the newsmen who chose the winners racists and threatening to leave North Carolina for his senior year. Later he calmed down a bit, somewhat softening his stand: "Maybe I was being selfish and egotistical and bull-headed like some people think. Maybe in retrospect the awards could have gone either way. But I just thought we had done so much for the conference that we deserved some special recognition. Why didn't we get it? Well, you tell me why.

"But I'm not sorry I spoke up, even if people don't like me for it. It's okay for sportswriters to say what they think, but for some reason people don't like to hear athletes speak up. That's why I don't think I'll ever be Player of the Year now. They'll remember this. But maybe by talking up I can prevent this from happening to someone else. I don't consider it so much an injustice to me as an injustice to black athletes and black people everywhere. I've been trying to tell them there is no prejudice in the ACC—how do you explain this?"

Charlie did return to North Carolina for his senior year, leading the Tar Heels into the National Invitational Tourney with a 27.1 scoring average. By the end of the season, pro scouts from both leagues were waiting for his decision.

Scott would have been a great catch for any NBA team. But for the struggling ABA, he could be a league-saver. Too many famous college players had turned their backs on the younger league. That very preseason the ABA lost Pete Maravich, college ball's most publicized senior. The Washington Caps, the ABA team that won the draft rights to Scott, put an extra effort into signing him. They offered two big incentives: one, a six-figure contract (undisclosed); and two, the fact that they played their home games in the nation's capital—a big plus for a man who planned to study law in the offseason, as Charlie did. Scott went with the ABA.

Then before his rookie year (1970–71), the Caps became the Virginia Squires, a regional franchise playing in various cities around that state. Charlie lost the possible advantages of playing in Washington, but he soon established himself as the best guard in the league. A lanky 6-foot-6, he stopped other guards cold on defense with his sheer height advantage. On offense his moves were so quick and his shooting so accurate that he astounded everyone. "Charlie right now may be the best all-round player in either league," said teammate Ray Scott (no relation) late in the season. Ray Scott had seen nine years of duty in the NBA, so he knew what he was talking about. "Charlie has no equal in driving to the basket," he continued. "He reminds me a lot of Dave Bing. Charlie has such great versatility and, above all, is a great team player."

Scott had some great rookie games with the Squires. One night, in a match with their Eastern Division rivals the Kentucky Colonels, Charlie came off the bench—where he was taking one of his rare breathers—to score 14 points in one minute and 58 seconds to win the game 147–135. In a game against the Floridians, he assured a Virginia victory by hitting eight straight field goals in the fourth quarter—lay-ups, hooks, jumpers.

Scott was happy with his choice of leagues at the time. "Man," he chattered enthusiastically, "the ABA is a guard's league. I'll admit the NBA has it over us because we don't have the real good big men in quantity, but we've got great guards. Oscar Robertson and Jerry West in the NBA are super guards. But Bob Verga, Larry Jones, Louie Dampier, Levern Tart—those guys can play for anybody. We've got tall ones, short ones and midisized ones. Every ABA club is tough at guard. If I want to test myself, the ABA is the place."

Scott wound up his rookie season third in league scoring with a 27.1 average. He was number one in controversy, however. Some of the criticism of his behavior at Chapel Hill had followed him into the ABA. It was never Charlie's style to keep silent about anything that troubled him. For instance, he spoke out on what he considered poor officiating. He also complained about what he considered unfair treatment of black athletes by management and press.

Nevertheless, the writers couldn't ignore his skill. He was chosen co-Rookie of the Year along with Dan Issel of the Colonels. The Squires breezed to an Eastern Division crown, and Scott averaged better than 26 points a game in the twelve playoff contests that followed.

Charlie got off to a fast start in 1971–72. So fast, that he took over the scoring lead in the first month of play and never lost it. But though he was scoring more, he was beginning to enjoy it less. One problem was that he had to put up the ball more often because of injuries to other starters. It was not unusual to see him attempt 30 field goals a game. During one eleven-game stretch he scored 40 or more points every night. Sensational rookie Julius Erving controlled the boards and aided in the scoring while Scott guided the offense and took on the point-making burden. The Squires became a kind of two-man circus. Yet, basketball is supposed to be a five-man sport. The Squires started to run a poor second to Kentucky in the East.

Scott's critics came out in full force. They claimed he was trying to hog the show, that he was more interested in getting his points than in seeing his team win. "If I felt I was hurting the club, I would cut down on my shooting," Scott answered them. "In fact, when all our injured players get back to par, I'll probably be shooting less."

"Examine it from my side," he went on. "I've never won a scoring title, except for one in the ACC, and I don't expect to win one this year. If I score 40 and we win, naturally I'm happy. If I score 20 and we win I'm just as happy. But if we lose, man, the feeling is one of emptiness."

The criticism got harsher as the season progressed. The injured players didn't come back as expected. And pressure on the team mounted. Virginia was losing too many games to the league's weakest teams. The Squires, always a physical team, became even more so to make up for the lack of balance.

But angry fans didn't seem to see the other Virginia players when the action got rough. All they saw was Charlie Scott. "Scott's always looking for a fight," complained one club owner. "He gets away with murder. He picks on everyone, and no one dares do anything about it. . . . Then too, he's so conceited."

Charlie began to feel a strong disenchantment with the whole situation. One day, near his Norfolk apartment, he told a reporter: "There's no social life here for a young black. There's nothing to do here, I stay in my apartment all the time. I'm like a share-cropper who comes in and works here, then cuts out after the harvest has been taken."

Scott felt that it was time to get out of the ABA. He had been secretly negotiating with the Phoenix Suns of the NBA. They offered him more money than he was getting with Virginia. Perhaps he felt they also offered an escape from the criticism and the bad-mouthing he was getting with the Squires. Anyway, in 1972 he jumped to the NBA after playing 73 games in the 84-game season. All he left the league was a league-leading 34.5-point scoring average.

The news of his defection shocked the pro basketball world. Charlie had to go to court to win the legal right to play for the Suns, but he appeared in their last six games of the season. The Phoenix fans anticipated Scott's first full year in the NBA, and he didn't disappoint them.

Unfortunately controversy followed him over from the ABA. The Suns were a struggling, mistake-prone team. They played as five individuals without a leader rather than as a smooth unit. Part of the problem was that only forward Connie Hawkins and guard Dick Van Arsdale were used to each other's moves. Center Neal Walk was a new starter, forward Gus Johnson had just come from Baltimore and Scott's role was that of scorer, rather than play-maker.

Charlie bore the blame that might more justly have been spread over the entire team. It was a familiar refrain: he was too busy making points to

When Charlie jumped to the NBA Phoenix Suns in 1972, the new competition included superstars like the Big O, Oscar Robertson (#1).

make the plays the Suns so badly needed. The criticism got even stronger when Phoenix coach Butch van Breda Kolff was fired in October. Van Breda Kolff claimed that one of the reasons he was sacked was that he had tried too hard to limit Charlie's shots and increase his assists. Apparently the Suns' ownership liked the tall guard just the way he was.

As the year progressed, however, the Suns found even more reason to like their new guard. As soon as he adjusted to the team, Charlie's scoring began to drop a bit while his assists began to rise. At midseason Scott was named to the NBA's first All-Star team, and by the end of the season he was averaging more than 25 points and better than six assists per game.

So after all the heat, Charlie Scott had finally emerged as a bright spot on the Suns.

9.

Gus Johnson

In 1963 Baltimore rookie Gus Johnson entered the NBA with a bang. In a preseason exhibition game with San Francisco, the new Bullet drove on veteran Guy Rodgers, took off at the foul line and soared to the basket. Rodgers, in a desperate attempt to stop Gus, grabbed hold of him—and was carried aloft all the way to the target. Despite his passenger, Johnson slammed the ball through the net. The weight of the two men broke the hoop.

After the game a newsman asked Gus if he were as strong as he looked. "Stronger," was the reply.

Throughout his career Gus Johnson was a tower of strength. At 6-foot-5 and 235 pounds, he wasn't big for an NBA forward. Yet the power in his arms and legs surpassed that of most of his

The clean-up crew puts things back together again after a Gus Johnson special!

larger opponents. But strength was only one facet of his game. Gus had fantastic body control—the kind of agility and coordination that made him, in the words of one writer, "the greatest midair performer in basketball." His sweet, spectacular moves earned him the nickname "Honeycomb."

In his prime, Johnson was one of the most dazzling performers in the league. Injuries slowed him down in later years, but in the good old days—his college and early pro years—people watched Gus play with awe. Joe Cipriano, Johnson's coach at the University of Idaho, recalled a game in which Gus made a rebound play that astounded everyone present. Johnson, he said, "grabbed the ball above the rim, with his back to the board. Before he came down, he spun around and threw a behind-the-back pass that traveled three-quarters the length of the court. It caught a forward in stride, and the guy laid it up."

Of course, that kind of skill didn't come overnight. Gus was an all-round athlete at Central High in Akron, Ohio. He excelled in football, basketball and the high jump. Johnson's gridiron style as a linebacker was so reckless and so brutal that his teammates dubbed him "Bloody Gus." When he broke a knee during a game, he decided to make basketball his main sport.

As a basketball player Gus was simply great. He shot accurately, played admirable defense and jumped so well that he was picked to play center his senior year. And it wasn't because the team lacked big men, either. One of Johnson's teammates was a 6-foot-8 forward named Nate Thurmond, who later became the Golden State Warriors' center.

Playing for Central High, Gus made the kind of passes that brought gasps from the crowd. If a man was open, Johnson would get the ball to him. "I had—what d'ya call it?—peripheral vision, and when I let those passes go, I could *feel* where the man was." Johnson helped his peripheral vision along by drilling on his own for hours at a time. His favorite exercise was throwing blind passes at a white spot he had painted on a wall.

Dozens of college recruiters approached Johnson, but he just wasn't interested. He didn't mind the idea of playing college ball, but he'd had his fill of schoolwork. At that time Gus had no real ambition. After graduation he spent most of his time haunting the poolhalls in Akron's black section. As he told it: "All I wanted to do was hang out with the fellows and shoot pool. I was one of the best pool players in Akron. I'd borrow a couple of dollars from my mother and stay at the poolroom till it closed. One night I borrowed five from her and won $300 and came home and threw it on the bed. My mother said, 'Where'd you get that?' When I told her, she didn't like that. She's a real religious woman."

Somewhere along the line, Gus decided to give college a try and enrolled in the University of Akron. He played freshman ball, but instead of hitting the books, he spent his off-court time in the poolhall hitting the side pocket. After one semester he dropped out and got a job. But that didn't last long, either. He soon found he could make more money with less work bending over a billiard table.

One day Johnson was approached by a man named George Swyers, who was a close friend of Joe Cipriano, the coach at the University of Idaho. Swyers wanted Gus to go to a junior college for a year and then join Cipriano's team. Johnson listened with disbelief. "I thought Swyers was crazy," Johnson recalled. "I was livin' good. I had my own car. I lived with my parents. I didn't want for anything. So why should I go to school?" As strange as Swyers' suggestion seemed at first, once the idea was planted in Gus' mind he couldn't seem to get it out. Thinking of his past—and his future—Johnson began to realize that unless he got away from Akron and got an education, he might spend the rest of his life in poolhalls. So he packed his bags and spent the next year as a student at Boise Junior College in Idaho. Gus had married his hometown girlfriend before leaving Akron, so the newlyweds rented an apartment near the campus. The largely white environment was alien but friendly.

Boise's coach, George Blankly, had gotten the word on Gus' fine skills from Swyers and Cipriano, but he was still skeptical. The first time he got Gus into the gym Blankly asked him: "Can you shoot? Can you hook?"

"Which hand?" Gus replied.

137

GUS JOHNSON

Thinking that Johnson was just boasting, the coach shrugged and said, "Okay, the left hand."

Johnson stepped back until he was 25 feet from the basket—and swished in a left-handed hook. Blankly's eyes bugged. Then, without a word, Gus tossed in a perfect right-handed hook.

Gus was very happy at Boise. He starred on the basketball team and buckled down to his studies. And the next year he transferred to the University of Idaho as planned. Under coach Cipriano, Gus continued to play super ball. He finished the 1962–63 season as the nation's second-best collegiate rebounder. The local papers raved about him, claiming they had a real "Globetrotter" on the team.

But Idaho didn't have its "Globetrotter" for long. All the publicity young Gus received reached the ears of the pro scouts. Although Johnson still had another year to go at Idaho, four years had passed since he started college at Akron. Therefore, under the NBA's bylaws he became "draftbait," eligible for pro duty.

Several pro teams contacted Johnson, and Baltimore picked him up on the second round of the 1963 draft. So, with less than three seasons of college ball behind him, Johnson signed with Baltimore and entered the big league.

As a Baltimore rookie in 1963, Johnson's high-flying style made him an instant favorite with the Bullet fans.

GUS JOHNSON

The Bullets gave him $15,000 to sign—not much by today's high standards. But Gus didn't quibble over his salary because he was confident that he could quickly become a star player and make big money fast. He even bragged to his pals that he would break the league open with his style.

Gus did show some flashes of brilliance, but still he spent the early part of his rookie year getting shown up by the older and wiser vets, who rapidly adjusted to his free-wheeling ways. As a result, the young rookie became nervous and started to press too hard. He was shocked to find himself making all kinds of mistakes. One day he was so depressed he asked coach Bob Leonard if he really belonged in the league. "If I didn't believe you could do the job," the Baltimore coach snapped, "you wouldn't be out there starting."

Things gradually changed for the better, and Johnson regained his original swagger. He learned how to blend with his teammates and still play his own game. Soon he was a favorite of the fans. They loved to watch him execute between-the-legs passes, block countless plays and toss in seemingly impossible shots. Gus' body control was so great that he often appeared to be hanging in midair, as if suspended by invisible wires.

After a shaky start, Johnson finished his first pro year with a 17.3 points-per-game scoring average and better than twelve rebounds a game. "I'm a crowd pleaser," he said to sportswriters. "Some of the things I do sometimes amaze me. I don't see how I do them."

It seemed the only thing Gus couldn't do was win the Rookie of the Year award. That prize went to Jerry Lucas of the Cincinnati Royals. Gus was particularly upset because since high school he had been engaged in a sort of impersonal rivalry with Lucas. While Johnson was starring at Central High, Lucas was gaining all-state honors at Middletown High, some miles away. And while Johnson was relatively isolated at Idaho, Lucas was an All-America on the Ohio State team, a contender for the national championship. Coming into the league Gus rode a ripple compared to the tidal-wave of Lucas' publicity. Johnson felt the award had been decided in Jerry's favor before the season even began. "They didn't know anything about Gus Johnson," he complained bitterly.

Being ignored was a particularly painful experience for Johnson, and a new one. He had always been a colorful character—dashing, exotic, eccentric—the kind of person who seldom went unnoticed on or off the court. As a teenager he had sported a goatee and worn a gold gypsy earring in one ear. Gus always dressed in expensive, tailormade clothes and threw money around as if the supply was inexhaustible.

And then there was his famous false tooth. In an overly enthusiastic intrasquad scrimmage, center Walt Bellamy broke one of Gus' front teeth.

"The Bell and I had had some differences," Johnson recalled, "and then I came in for a lay-up and his elbow caught me and busted my tooth in half. I had to get a new one so I decided I wanted a design on it. This just came to me." The artificial tooth Gus chose had a bright gold star imbedded in it. "A star for a star," he explained. "It fits my character."

Gus was always very certain—and very vocal—about his own worth. When it was time to negotiate a new contract, he told the press: "I know I'm a drawing card. When people come to see the Bullets, they come to see Gus Johnson. It's time the club realized it."

Actually, part of Johnson's boasting was just a put-on. He liked to shock the press by stepping outside the mold of the "humble" athlete. But Gus was always very popular with fans, teammates and the newsmen.

In his second pro season Johnson's feats became even more spectacular. During a game in St. Louis, he made one of his patented stuff shots, completely shattering the backboard. The match was delayed for 25 minutes while the backboard was replaced, and one player had to sit out the rest of the game because the flying hoop hit him on the foot. Gus recounted the story with glee: "The announcer said, 'This has got to be the strongest man in the NBA. He breaks one basket a year.' You could hear the people saying, 'Look how strong he

Gus Johnson: "a star for a star."

is.' I was walking around with my chest out. The guys were calling me Hercules."

Johnson ended the 1964–65 season with an average of 18.6 points and 13 rebounds a game. He was making steady progress toward superstardom when bad luck struck. He bruised his left wrist in a preseason match in 1965. It hurt him a bit but didn't seem too serious. Then, during the second game of the regular season, he collided with his old rival Jerry Lucas (against whom he always gave a little extra) and reinjured the same wrist. This time there was a lot of pain. The wrist swelled up like a football. It wasn't broken, but there was damage to the nerve that ran along one of the bones. It took a three-hour operation to fix it.

Gus appeared in only 42 games in the 1965–66 season. Yet, he was tough enough and good enough to be named second team All-NBA at the end of the year. Considering how little he played that year, it was a very unusual honor—a tribute to his prowess. Gus deserved the praise. Paul Seymour, the Baltimore coach that year, estimated that Johnson's absence cost the team eight to ten victories.

Johnson quickly proved his value when he returned to action later in the season, helping the Bullets beat the Lakers, 123–121, with 26 points and 16 rebounds. His one-on-one antics demoralized Los Angeles. At one point in the game, Johnson, guarded by Elgin Baylor, took a pass and leaped for the basket. Suddenly, while swooping through the air, he lost control of the ball. It fell from his right hand, rolling down his arm to his elbow. But that didn't stop Gus. He simply hit the ball with his elbow, guiding it into the hoop for two points.

Despite such crowd-thrilling heroics, Johnson received his share of criticism. The main argument against him was his inconsistency. Kevin Loughery, who was then Johnson's teammate, answered that charge: "It's kind of an unfair rap. A guy who is flashy and exciting always gets this rap because people are disappointed if he doesn't make the fantastic stuff shot every game."

Gus himself admitted there was some merit to the criticism. "I'm inconsistent," he agreed. "But when my shooting is off, I try to concentrate on other parts of the game—defense, setting picks, rebounding. There's a lot more to basketball than scoring."

Few men played a better all-round game than Gus. The majority of pro players fall into two categories: one-on-one artists (strong on offense, weak on defense) and muscle men (strong on defense, weak on offense). A relative handful of stars have combined both strengths. Gus Johnson was such a player. His defense was tough, and his offense was tricky. When he was healthy, Johnson could duel the huskiest muscle men in the league to a standstill. Fans filled arenas to watch him battle for rebounds with Dave DeBusschere, Bill Bridges, Paul Silas and Jerry Lucas.

Gus knew his defense. "It's more than just playing head-up on your man," he explained. "First you have to try and keep him from getting the ball. You play between your man and the ball. Once your man gets the ball, you overplay him to the left or right to force him to his weaker side or force him to go where you can get help from your big man. Finally, after he gets off his shot, you get him on your back and box him out so he can't follow up. The key is determination."

Determination and recklessness. Johnson's de-
tractors said he played too hard. Even Kevin
Loughery once said, "Moving your body around in
the air, you've got to come down in awkward positions. To play the game the way Gus does, I think
you've got to get hurt."

Ironically, it was Loughery who was involved in
Johnson's biggest injury, which occurred during
the 1968–69 season. Although injuries had plagued
Gus' entire career, this one changed his whole life.
In February 1969 he collided with Loughery on a
fast break, severely damaging the cartilage in his
knee. Johnson was never quite the same after that.
Gus missed the remainder of the 1968–69 season,
then had an operation which allowed him to play
the next year. But the knee had lost much of its
flexibility. It continued to hurt him and fill up with
fluid that had to be drawn out with a long needle
before each game. No one actually said that Gus
was washed up, but everywhere there were whis-
pers that the old Gus was gone.

In 1969–70, Johnson still averaged 17.3 points a
game and pulled down 1,086 rebounds. He looked
good in the playoffs although the Bullets finally fell
to the Knicks after seven torrid games. Gus averaged 18.4 points in those games, holding Dave De-
Busschere to 14.6 points a game.

But things got worse in the 1970–71 season.
Gus' other knee became inflamed—not through an

accident but through ordinary wear and tear. In fact, his right knee started giving him more trouble than his left. It needed more care, hurt more and swelled up much more. He still managed to play in 66 games and had a good year with 18.2 points per game and 1,128 rebounds. By playoff time, however, Gus was in total agony. He couldn't sleep at night because of the pain. There was also a great deal of psychological pain and worry.

The Bullets went on to the NBA final playoff round against the Bucks. The only action Gus saw in that series was as a substitute, and Milwaukee crushed Baltimore in four straight games.

In May 1971, Johnson had surgery on both knees, but in 1971–72 he was still a sub. Early in the season an optimistic Bullet spokesman claimed, "It's a matter of his working himself back into shape for the playoffs."

But the 1971–72 season was not a good one for Gus. He appeared in only 39 matches, averaging 6.4 points per game. Needless to say, he wasn't ready for the playoffs. Baltimore was defeated by New York in six games. Johnson played a total of 77 minutes in the series and averaged just four points a game.

Those statistics were the worst in Johnson's career. It was time for him to take a serious look at his future. A change had to be made, for he was of little value to the Bullets. It came as no surprise to Johnson when Baltimore traded him to Phoenix for

In 1972–73, Gus joins a new league and a new team—the ABA Pacers.

a second-round pick in the NBA draft after the playoffs.

Gus worked hard to get in shape for the 1972–73 season in Phoenix, and his efforts paid off. He was made a spot starter on his new team. His knees held up, allowing him to shoulder much of the team's rebounding. And playing with high point-makers Charlie Scott and Connie Hawkins meant he no longer had to worry about his scoring.

By December, however, the mediocre Suns decided they needed even more scoring punch in their line-up. Guard Dick Van Arsdale was moved up front, and Gus became the extra man at forward. Johnson—who was then averaging about nine points a game—was put on waivers.

Several teams in both leagues were interested in him, but Gus decided to sign with the ABA's Indiana Pacers. Johnson's choice was influenced by the fact that the Pacers were being coached by Bob Leonard, the man who had been his first coach at Baltimore.

Although he was still a sub, Johnson's experience was highly valued by the Pacers. He worked closely with the team's fine young cornermen, George McGinnes and Darrell Hillman.

"Gus has been a great influence here," said coach Leonard. "That's on and off the court. He's helped us in a lot of ballgames, and he's like my right-hand man."

INDEX

Page numbers in italics refer to photographs.